DATE DUE

FEB 16 1993	JAN 2 9 2001	
6/4/93 ILL	FEB 1 6 2001	
	OCT 0 6 2001	
NOV 2 2 1993	MAR 2 9 2004	
MAY 2 3 1994	MAY 1 1 2004	
NOV 2 3 1994	JUL 2 8 2005	
MAY 2 6 1995	DEC 1 5 2009	
NOV 9 1995		
DEC 2 6 1995 FEB 1 2 1996		
DEC 2 1996 DEC 1 1997		
MAR 2 0 1999		
OCT 2 6 1999		

Demco, Inc. 38-293

Introducing the Manatee ∽

Mermaids and mermen cast in bronze grace the pedestal of Queen Victoria's monument in front of Buckingham Palace, London. Exquisite detail and the strength and vitality of the sculptures prepare the mind to accept what is only a dream. Photos by the author.

Introducing the Manatee

WARREN ZEILLER

UNIVERSITY PRESS OF FLORIDA

Gainesville / Tallahassee / Tampa / Boca Raton
Pensacola / Orlando / Miami / Jacksonville

Copyright 1992 by the Board of Regents of the State of Florida

Printed in the United States of America on acid-free paper ∞

All rights reserved

The University Press of Florida is the scholarly publishing agency for the State University System of Florida, comprised of Florida A & M University, Florida Atlantic University, Florida International University, Florida State University, University of Central Florida, University of Florida, University of North Florida, University of South Florida, and University of West Florida.

University Press of Florida
15 Northwest 15th Street
Gainesville, FL 32611

Library of Congress Cataloging-in-Publication Data

Zeiller, Warren, 1929-
    Introducing the manatee / Warren Zeiller.
        p.   cm.
    Includes bibliographical references and index.
    ISBN 0–8130–1152–3
    1. Manatees.   I. Title.
QL737.S63Z45   1992   92–9326
599.5'5—dc20   CIP

Quotations from *The Captive Sea* by Craig Phillips (©1964 by the author) are used with the permission of the Chilton Book Company, Radnor, Pennsylvania.

Miami Seaquarium® is the registered trademark of Wometco Enterprises, Inc. of Coral Gables, Florida, and is recognized here in order to avoid redundancy throughout the text of this book.

Contents ⚏

A bogus mermaid. As P. T. Barnum might have said, "a genuine curiosity of Natural History collected from the farthest reaches of the mysterious Orient!" This mermaid was ingeniously constructed of fish skin and scales, its carved wooden body topped with a woolly crown, and embellished with frightful nails and teeth. Photo courtesy of Miami Seaquarium.

Preface ☙

Throughout the ancient world, myths of a race of beings uniting the forms of human and fish persisted for centuries. Noah (known as second father of the human race and preserver and teacher of the arts and sciences before the great flood), his wife and his three sons all were depicted as fish-tailed deities. Philistines and Babylonians called this human-fish Dagon; in legends of India it is Vishnu and may be visualized in the form of a person issuing from the mouth of a fish rather than as a part of it. The Syrian goddess Atergatis, also a fish divinity, conferred upon her people strict rules for conservation of their fisheries. She was worshiped by the Greeks as Astarte or Derceto. With the fish portion of her body discarded, she became the celestial Aphrodite, known to Cyprians and Romans as Venus and regarded as the representative of the reproductive power of nature. The discarded fish portion of her body was allotted to lesser deities called Tritons. Depicted as both males and females, Tritons rendered homage and service to Venus and were powerful in their own right as sea gods.

The human-fish or siren form has thus been known to almost all generations as an object of religious worship. The belief was reinforced by visual depictions—coins, medals, pictures, and sculptures—and became accepted as reality. Preconditioned by these ideas, early mariners were quite prepared to encounter mermaids or mermen in visible and tangible forms at sea. The life forms in which they found their mermaids were dugongs and manatees, the Sirenians.

This work is dedicated to ancient mariners whose mind's eye perceived Sirenian grace and wondrous beauty in mermaids of the sea.

Before moving to Florida, I had encountered only mythical sirens in high school English literature. In Florida in 1960, I was introduced to the living progenitors of the mermaid myth, the manatees or sea cows. My work has included them ever since. When two adult manatees were entrusted to my care, their successful maintenance was a frustrating day-to-day learning experience because of the dearth of data on these fascinating aquatic herbivores. Searches of the literature uncovered little more than the same generalizations, repeated over and over. Scientific investigation of Sirenians was stimulated by passage of the Marine Mammal Act of 1972 and the Endangered Species Act of 1973. As data became more available I felt that what there was should be pulled together to fill the void. Where information was not yet in print or seemed unobtainable, correspondence with researchers in the field never failed to yield less than complete cooperation. Other aspects of this text have been taken from historical writings as well as from my own experience.

Manatees rapidly are nearing extinction and few people seem to care, but not because of insensitivity. They simply are no more aware than was I many years ago. This work is intended to share with the reader everything of substance I have learned about Sirenians . . . whose only predator is man.

I wish to express my gratitude to those people throughout the world who have shared with me their experiences, time, data, and photographs on behalf of this work: W. L. E. de Alwis, B.Sc., F.Z.E., National Zoological Gardens of Sri Lanka; Alan Baldridge, Rosenstiel School of Marine and Atmospheric Science, University of Miami, Florida; Daniel K. Odell, Ph.D., Sea World of Florida, Orlando, Florida; G. C. L. Bertram, Ph.D., chair, I.U.C.N. Survival Service Commission, St. John's College, Cambridge, England; Colonel J. J. Brown and Major Lewis W. Shelfer, Jr., Florida Marine Patrol, Department of Natural Resources, Tallahassee, Florida; Howard Campbell and Blair Irvine, National Fish and Wildlife Laboratory, Gainesville, Florida; Stephen L. Cumbaa and Elizabeth Wing, Ph.D., the Florida Museum of Natural History, University of Florida, Gainesville; Daryl P. Doming, Ph.D., Howard University, Washington, D.C.; Leonard J. Grant, associate secretary, National Geographical Society; George E. Heinsohn, Ph.D., James Cook University of North Queensland, Australia; Charles H. Hoessle, general curator/deputy director, St. Louis Zoological Park, Missouri; Sandra Hussar and James J. Mead, curator of marine mammals, National Museum of Natural History, and S. Dillon Ripley, secretary, Smithsonian Institution, Washington, D.C.; Teruo Kataoka, Toba Aquarium, Japan; Diana Magor, Instituto Nacional de Pesquisas da Amazonia, Manaus, Brazil; E. Mondolfi, FUDENA; Lawrence J. Nunn, Flood Control District, West Palm Beach, Florida; Electa Pace, Marine Films-Medifilms, Boca Raton, Florida; Sandra Peterson, Santa Monica, California; P. Craig Phillips, director, National Aquarium, Washington, D.C.; David C. Powell, assistant superintendent, Steinhart

Aquarium, California Academy of Sciences, San Francisco; Barbara A. Purdy, Ph.D., assistant professor, anthropology and social sciences, University of Florida, Gainesville; George D. Ruggieri, director, Osborn Laboratories of Marine Science, Brooklyn, N.Y.; F. G. Walton Smith, Ph.D., president, International Oceanographic Foundation, Miami, Florida; Noel D. Vietmeyer, Ph.D., National Academy of Sciences, Washington, D.C.; and Bernard Yokel, Ph.D., executive director, Florida Audubon Society, Maitland, Florida.

Sirens Sing Ever More Softly 〰

Baby Manatees
at Seaquarium

Manatee births in the wild invariably occur in secluded, out-of-the-way places and without witnesses. Therefore, when births take place in zoos, aquariums, or oceanariums they offer serious educational opportunities as well as public relations boons. When the creatures involved are of an endangered species, the potential is of immeasurable importance.

In 1957 at the Miami Seaquarium a female manatee was born to a dam who had been brought in pregnant from the wild. Several years later an account of this event and of the stories surrounding it were recorded in *The Captive Sea* by Seaquarium's first curator, Craig Phillips.

During the time that we were setting up the tide pool exhibit, I received a phone call from a resident of Key Biscayne, several miles away, informing me that there was what appeared to be a motherless baby manatee, or sea cow, swimming about the boat harbor there. The caller wondered if we might be able to capture and care for it. On being told that it was very tiny, just over 3 feet long, and that it was staying close to the side of a boat tied to the dock, I got together with Captain Gray, who headed our collecting operations, to make plans for the little creature's capture.

We placed a large mattress and a blanket in the back of our truck, and I donned my swimming trunks while Gray selected an oversize dipnet with heavy mesh and a long handle. On arriving at the dock in the truck, we saw that the little manatee was in bad shape; it was quite emaciated from lack of food and its back showed injuries where some senseless person had tried unsuccessfully to spear it. On becoming aware of our presence, the manatee dove beneath the boat, and we presumed that it would soon surface on the other side. Since we lacked access to that side of the boat it was decided that I would enter the water a short distance away and would swim as carefully as possible toward the boat from the far side, herding the manatee within range of the net.

When I approached the boat, however, the manatee was nowhere in sight. I called to Captain Gray who was on the dock beyond my sight, asking if it might have swum back under the boat, but he saw no sign of it. I decided to explore beneath the boat, and so, adjusting my face mask and taking a deep breath, I submerged slowly so as to create as little disturbance as possible. The water was fairly clear, and although I could easily see along the keel of the boat and beyond its stern, there was no sign of the little sea cow.

Slowly I turned around to face toward the bow of the boat, and suddenly there was the padlike, bristly snout of the manatee, as it looked straight at me with slightly quizzical Weakeyes-Yokum expression, not 6 inches from my face mask! It seemed quite unafraid; and so, rather than attempt to drive it out in the open where it might conceivably escape, I decided to try to capture it myself. With a sudden motion I flung both arms around its middle and hugged it tightly against my chest. Since it was noticeably weak and starved, I had little trouble holding it, and I recall that it emitted several tiny plaintive squeaks as it struggled underwater. Breaking surface on dock side with the little manatee held securely in my arms, I shouted to Gray, who reached down and hoisted it up by its flippers. We laid the manatee down carefully on the mattress, covered it with a wet blanket and drove back to the aquarium, where we placed it for the time being in a large wooden tank filled with seawater. . . .

Our little manatee, a female, had quite likely lost her mother . . . and her emaciated condition told us that chances of saving her life were none too good. I had no idea of the nutritional or physical qualities of manatee milk, but I promptly sent for a veterinarian in the hope that between us we could think of something in the way of a substitute diet. While I was awaiting his arrival a most fortunate coincidence occurred.

I had lifted the little manatee from its tank (it weighed only 27 pounds) and set it on a mattress, where I carefully painted each spear wound with antiseptic. I was bending over it feeling relieved that its injuries appeared to be merely superficial, thanks to its tough hide, when I gradually became aware that two people were standing beside me, watching. Looking up, I saw Dr. Donald de Sylva of the Marine Laboratory and beside him stood an attractive young woman with dark hair. "Craig," said de Sylva, "I want you to meet Eugenie Clark."

Here was the one person who could help me! Dr. Clark, whose famous book "Lady with a Spear" I had recently read, is an eminent marine biologist who had made an extensive study, among other things, of dugongs in the Red Sea. She told us that the milk of the dugong, and almost certainly that of the manatee, was extremely thick in consistency, in fact, nearly a solid. This was something to go on, and in consulting with

Captain William B. Gray (*left*), Seaquarium director of collections and exhibits, and curator Craig Phillips (*right*) test baby's willingness to suckle; she was more than willing, but the nipple was weak. Ingenuity prevailed, and calf pail and nipple provided the solution. When found she was thought to be about three weeks old; she was starving and had suffered spear wounds in her back. Photo courtesy of Miami Seaquarium.

the vet, I decided to try condensed milk thickened with Pablum, with a little cod-liver oil and corn syrup mixed in.

The manatee had shown a willingness to suckle from the first, when I experimentally poked my finger in its mouth, and I noticed that on capture its nose was reddened with copper paint, where it had repeatedly nuzzled the bottom of the boat.

We gave it its first meal from a baby's nursing bottle which I had purchased from a nearby pharmacy, and, although it readily took the nipple, it seemed to have difficulty in drawing the thick liquid through, even though we had enlarged the hole. My solution was to obtain a calves' nursing pail from a local dairy supplier, and to this was attached a specially large nipple with a check valve inside. I had a 10-inch length of pipe welded on between the nipple attachment and the pail outlet, and this made it possible for the baby to nurse underwater and at the same

Baby manatee feeding from nursing bucket. Courtesy of Craig
Phillips.

time breathe when the pail was fastened to the edge of the tank, since its
valvular nostrils were located on the very top of its snout.

Thanks to this feeding device and to Dr. Clark's helpful advice, our
manatee continued to get milk regularly, although after a week's time it
was still very thin and had gained weight only slightly. Then it abruptly
ceased feeding, and although we continued to give it vitamin injections
and attempted to force milk into its stomach with a tube, it died 10 days
after we had caught it.

Of course, attempting to raise an animal about which so little is
known to date would be tricky business under the most favorable conditions, but I still feel our chances of success would have been much better
had we been able to capture it a little sooner. However, during the brief
time it survived in our care I was able to learn a little concerning its habits,
and this information, along with additional observations I was able to
make on captive manatees elsewhere, later proved highly useful when we
eventually obtained an adult female for the Seaquarium two years later.

We named her Cleopatra because she was so beautiful. Her body was
fresh and glistening as she emerged from the river, and her breath came
forth in a languid sigh. Her skin was gray and pebble-toned and covered
all over with delicate, silky hairs. Her eyes were minute, black, and oozed
gluey tears as she watched me, and her lips shuddered slightly, for they
were dragging on the ground. This was the moment I had long awaited;
she was in the net, the most beautiful sea cow I had ever seen!

Ever since the loss of our baby manatee I had hoped that we might
secure another specimen for the Seaquarium. Since they are rigidly protected by law, it was necessary to obtain a special permit from the Florida
State Board of Conservation, and having secured this, it was necessary to
wait for some time in order to locate a suitable specimen that could be
captured—or, rather, in a location where it could be netted, since this was
an impossibility in most of the jagged rock-walled canals where they were
to be found.

Cleo. Courtesy of Craig
Phillips.

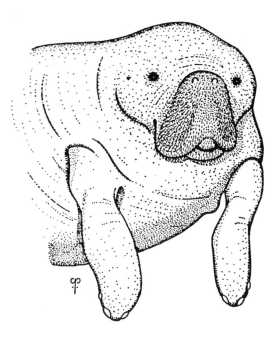

We had made a number of unsuccessful attempts to net an immense
sea cow that paid periodic visits to the Seaquarium boat slip on the rising
tide. Unfortunately, this old-timer was far too wary; we could never get
close to him, although we marveled at his vast brownish bulk adorned
with barnacles in the manner of a sea turtle. Although manatees normally
surface and blow silently, old Ferdinand, as we came to know him, would
snort in a manner that seemed absolutely contemptuous, and although
no gentler creature exists in the sea we knew we would really have our
hands full if we ever succeeded in surrounding him with a net (which we
were never able to do).

Once we managed to enclose a family of three that were browsing on
sea grass at the edge of a channel, but since the lead-line of our net rested
on soft mud, they easily worked their way under it and left in a great swirl
of mud. Another time we had a mother and calf enclosed in the net, but
the net filled with mud and grass and rolled under when we tried to raise
it, and again our quarry escaped.

I was becoming more and more impatient, because this was the main
item still lacking in our collection and we were becoming increasingly
aware of how difficult they were to secure. A dolphin is fairly easily entangled in a net because of its angular fins and flukes, but a manatee is a
rounded, blimp-like creature and nearly as difficult to snare as a bag of
wet cement.

Finally, one day in March, 1957, we received a phone call from some persons who had located a large manatee near the end of a system of canals that connect with the Miami River. Captain Gray and I drove out to investigate, and found the creature in a spot that made it appear available for capture—if only it would remain there long enough. Walking along the bank into a position far enough ahead of the manatee so as not to disturb it, I put on a face mask and fins and entered the water. I found the canal about 12 feet deep at that point and with a smooth bottom free from entanglement. It all looked quite promising, so we returned with the Seaquarium truck, a heavy net and plenty of extra help.

We knew we would have to move fast and enclose the manatee before it became frightened. One of our men swam across the canal as quickly as he could, dragging a long rope behind him, the other end of which was attached to the net. In no time at all we had our quarry bottled in, and seconds later the sea cow was in the bag of the net, pressing against it with so much force that the cork line was pulled completely beneath the surface. Giving the net some additional slack, we waited until the beast was thoroughly entangled, and then, with the help of a lifting crane we had hired for that purpose, we hoisted it into the bed of our truck, setting it carefully on a heavy mattress. On the return trip to Seaquarium I rode with her (she was a female) in the back of the truck. Moreover, she looked as if she were pregnant, and I was delighted over the possibility of an addition to our collection.

At the Seaquarium we again hoisted her, still wrapped in the net, into the shallow receiving flume between the two large tanks. As we cut the netting and freed her, she came to life in a spectacular manner (having lain nearly motionless in the truck), raising great waves as she swam about rapidly from one end of the flume to another. After a few minutes she quieted somewhat, although she remained quite nervous until dark, frequently rising to the surface to breathe.

Next morning, on arriving for work at the Seaquarium, I rushed up the stairs to the top deck to check on her condition. Our manatee was lying stiff and motionless on her back on the floor of the flume! I was dismayed. She seemed to be in such good shape the night before. Had she died of shock as some sea mammals do, or had she possibly suffered rough handling during capture? While I was pondering this, I thought I saw one of her flippers move perceptibly, and a moment later, still upside down, she began paddling languidly about the flume, finally rolling over to an upright position, coming up for several breaths of air, and then once again assuming her strange position of lifeless repose.

"Oh, NO!" exclaimed a voice from behind me. Turning around, I saw two of our tank divers who had just arrived on the scene, their faces the picture of tragedy. "What happened?" they asked. I turned away so they couldn't see that I was chuckling to myself, for I had just received the same shock. The manatee was swimming again, but by this time my companions had turned away to break the sad news to another person who was ascending the stairs. "Deader'n a doornail," said the first man, but his voice broke abruptly as he indicated our very much alive sea cow with a sweeping gesture of his hand.

Cleopatra was her name, soon shortened to Cleo, and we all became immensely fond of her. During the first few days of her captivity I spent considerable time in the flume with her, swimming alongside her, wearing a face mask. She was shy, but not too frightened at my presence, and when I was able to approach her closely enough to touch her, she would shudder slightly with a tiny, plaintive squeak and turn away. The sound was identical to that made by the first orphaned baby I had caught while the Seaquarium was still being built, and while almost inaudible at the surface, I could hear it very clearly underwater. The sound was made, as I have said, to the accompaniment of a slight shudder, but since no air bubbles were to be seen nor did the mouth appear to move, the sound must originate well back in the animal's throat.

Although I covered the surface of the flume with fresh lettuce and cabbage trimmings each night and cleaned them away each morning, there was no indication after a week's time that she had begun to feed. Moreover, she seemed to me to be losing weight and I was becoming worried. I was aware of the fact that captive sea cows are usually stubborn over shifting their diet to foods they are unused to. Paradoxically, Cleo's natural food, which consists of various marine and freshwater grasses, was growing in great abundance close to the Seaquarium, but it would be difficult to gather and terribly messy, besides, as considerable quantities of this rough forage would be required. It was unthinkable to attempt to fill the flume with all this wet hay, which would unavoidably drift into the main tanks.

Nonetheless, she was going to have to feed soon or risk starvation, so as an emergency measure I took a rake and a couple of tubs and gathered up a large quantity of Naias grass from a nearby canal. This is a fine, wispy, green waterweed often used to decorate home aquaria, and manatees consume large quantities of it whenever they can find it growing abundantly enough. As I placed bunches of the Naias in the flume I wondered if she would feed at all, for her digestive processes were in a state of temporary cessation. To my relief she started consuming it at once, and in the space of a minute had polished off the result of my hour and a half of work, and was looking around expectantly for more. Instead, I offered her some lettuce, which she scorned.

Cleo drinking from a hose.
Courtesy of Craig Phillips.

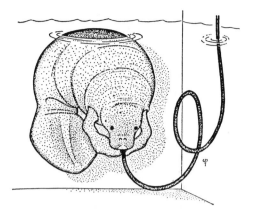

To keep her in Naias would require the full-time work of two men,
an obvious impracticability. I then turned to water hyacinths, a leathery
green plant whose air-filled floating leaves line the ditches and canals of
the Florida Everglades. She accepted the hyacinths as readily as she did
the Naias, so we began to make twice-weekly trips into the Everglades for
this staple until such time as we could wean her over to lettuce and
cabbage, which were easily obtainable from local markets.

Since manatees frequently leave the sea to travel up rivers (as Cleo
had done when we caught her) and there drink fresh water, I began to
wonder how Cleo was faring in this respect, being kept permanently in
full-salinity seawater. Certain marine reptiles and sea birds have salt
glands provided with ducts for the ejection of surplus body salt, but to my
knowledge nothing comparable is known to exist in the sea cow. Deciding
to see if she was interested, I attached a garden hose to a nearby tap,
turned on the water to low stream and dangled it into the flume so that the
water played across her nose. To my delight, Cleo took the hose in both
her flippers and held it against her mouth!

She was still having some difficulty manipulating it, but I found that if
the flow were cut down to just a slight trickle she could hold it with little
trouble. She drank water in this manner for almost a half hour before
dropping the hose. I began to water her every other day, and she would
rest on the bottom or in mid-water, holding the hose in her flippers from
five to ten minutes at a time. This performance was remarkably human to
behold, for the flippers of a manatee, though short and lacking fingers,
are jointed much as our own arms, and when they push grass into their
mouths or paddle themselves leisurely through the water, one can begin
to believe that these unfortunately dim-witted creatures may after all have
given rise to the legend of the mermaid.

I hate at this point to have to discourage romanticism in favor of cold
fact, but I must note that, while Cleo may have been a passable mermaid

in certain respects, in others she most definitely was not. I have seen drawings of female sea cows that were obviously executed by individuals whose imagination was greater than their factual observation, for they were depicted as having quite voluptuous breasts. Cleo, though mature and apparently gravid as well, could not, through any stretch of the imagination, be said to have a glamorous figure. In fact, in all the manatees that have come under my personal observation—and there have been quite a few—one really would have to look closely in order to distinguish the males from the females in this respect.

Returning to Cleo's manner of drinking water from a hose: this sight always seemed to baffle visitors to the aquarium. For some reason, it seemed implausible to them that she was drinking water while actually underwater herself. Repeatedly I would explain to curious onlookers that the kind of water she was drinking was not the same kind in which she was swimming. In fact, I remember that as a youngster in St. Petersburg I used to enjoy doing this very thing myself—sipping water from a hose while swimming beneath a dock, though I doubt that many others have indulged in this enjoyable pastime.

On one occasion, when I was watering Cleo, a somewhat cynical-looking gentleman walked up beside me and stared long and silently at the spectacle. Finally he turned in my direction and said, "Mind if I ask you a question?" "Not at all," I answered, prepared to deliver my customary dissertation on manatee hydraulics. "What are you putting into it?" he inquired. Something about the phrasing of his question deflected me from my usual response and with a straight face I answered, "Gasoline." For all I know, he may actually have believed me, for he merely nodded slightly and walked away.

Cleo prospered on her diet of water hyacinths, and the crumping noise the air floats made as she closed her jaws on them became a familiar sound in the flume. As I said before, the food of manatees is secured both with their flippers and their divided and highly mobile upper lip, which is covered with short bristles resembling the stubs of goose quills. There are no front teeth, chewing and grinding being done entirely by the heavy, flat rear molars. It is in the shape of the skull and the lower jaw especially that manatees resemble elephants, and the skin color, texture, and arrangement of hairs is also reminiscent of a young elephant. It is easy to look at the flattened flippers with their tiny flat nails and picture them as having evolved over the ages from the feet of the same river-browsing herbivore that gave rise to the mighty mastodons, mammoths, and modern elephants in a different direction.

Between her hyacinth meals and hose waterings, Cleo would leisurely paddle herself, often with just one flipper at a time, in a circular path around the flume, frequently pausing and "playing dead" on her back for a minute or so. Though I have observed a number of captive manatees before and since, I have never seen another one behave in this manner. Although she had apparently gained back the weight she lost while fasting, she did not appear to be quite so plump as during the first few days of her captivity, and at this time we fairly well abandoned the hope that she might be pregnant.

Eventually, it was time to move her from the flume to a new 15-by-30-foot oval tank which we had built for her from reinforced concrete on the Seaquarium grounds. We again had to tangle her in a section of netting and place her in a large metal and canvas cradle and lift her onto a mattress to a waiting truck, drive her to the new tank and slide her into the water. This was a process that she didn't enjoy in the least, and she softly squeaked her objections as we hoisted her great bulk from one tank to the other, her viscous tears—actually a secretion to protect her eyes from the wind—flowing freely. (I have read that the tears of her Indian Ocean relative, the dugong, are valued as a native love potion, though I cannot imagine how this tradition ever got started.)

Her tank was fitted with two separate water lines—one for fresh and one for salt water, so that we could supply her with any desired amount of salinity, and by alternating one kind of water with the other, we could retard the growth of algae as well. However, some algae still grew, not only on the sides of the tank, but also on Cleo's head, back and tail, so it was necessary to drain the water from the tank at intervals and go over the walls and Cleo herself with a heavy scrub brush. Later, it was discovered that the best remedy for this situation was to include several large mullet (*Mugil cephalus*) in the tank with the manatees, as they would keep the algae closely cropped at all times, and the manatees seemed to enjoy the fish "grazing" along their broad backs.

Likewise, Cleo appeared to enjoy her scrubbing. This was usually performed by one of the divers or tank attendants, but occasionally I would do this myself. Cleo was remarkably cooperative at this time, and even with the tank quite emptied of water she was easy to manage and would roll from her stomach to her back and over again at a slight nudging on my part. With a hose in one hand and a brush in the other I would often sit astride her back or flat tail while I scrubbed. Oddly enough, if there was enough water remaining in the tank to float her, Cleo usually objected to being handled. Often while lying on her back Cleo would cross her flippers on her chest, eyes closed, wearing all the while an inscrutably peaceful expression, and at such times I was tempted to place a white lily on her bosom for effect.

She would still eat nothing but water hyacinths, and her care was at this time turned over to Adolf Frohn, the Seaquarium's Director of Animal Training. Adolf was born in Germany of a family of professional animal trainers, and his great persistence, attention to detail, and devotion to his animals have won him some remarkable achievements and the renown of being the first man to successfully train the bottle-nosed dolphin in captivity.

Adolf's first undertaking was to induce Cleo to eat lettuce and cabbage, which she still stubbornly refused to do. Adolf had a square feeding tray made of 2 by 4 timber, which he floated in the tank in the same manner that a glass or plastic feeding ring is used in tropical fish tanks to prevent the too wide dispersion of floating food over the water surface.

Lettuce, cabbage, and hyacinth leaves were cut into small pieces, mixed together, and poured into the center of the ring. Cleo went for the food at once, and demonstrated a remarkable ability to manipulate the hyacinth portions into her mouth, leaving the rest untouched! Adolf chopped the portions finer and finer as time went by, patiently talking to Cleo and gently patting her as she fed, until at last she was accepting the lettuce and cabbage, which remained her diet from then on.

Cleo continued to thrive and be admired and photographed by hundreds of daily visitors, although she never became as tame as we had hoped. She was still reticent about being touched. She would, however, frequently feed from our hand, and visitors who were permitted to feed her enjoyed being tickled by her blunt quill-like bristles and always marveled at her tiny eyes and valvular nostrils, which were located on the very tip of her nose.

On August 27 came the exciting day. On arriving at work, I was informed that Cleo had given birth during the night and the tiny calf had been discovered by the watchman making his morning rounds! Had we but known, we might have observed or even photographed this event, which has never been witnessed and scientifically recorded. Only a short time before, we had decided that she was definitely *not* pregnant!

The small size of the calf at birth (35 pounds) had evidently fooled us. The baby stayed by its mother's side most of the time, although it would occasionally swim about at the surface of the tank. Its color was darker than that of Cleo herself, and its skin fairly soft at first, although this became rougher and more pebbly within a couple of days after birth.

I weighed the youngster (which proved to be a female) by lifting her out of the water and placing her in a large enameled pan on a scale. During this process, Cleo seemed not to mind our handling her baby, which was certainly one of the cutest baby mammals I had ever seen. It appeared to have had a very short umbilical cord, and I wondered if manatees, like dolphins, are normally born tail first in order that there be no danger of their drowning during the birth process.

Now in looking at Cleo I could see that the placement of her nipples, which were nearly in her armpits, made for a handy arrangement, for it seemed logically apparent that this would allow the baby to nurse and still be able to breathe at the same time the mother rose for air, which was usually about once a minute. However, for some reason we were to be forever thwarted in our attempts to witness the feeding technique, for at no time did we ever actually see Cleo feed her baby. Apparently this must occur quite rapidly and at very infrequent intervals (as it does in the case of rabbits, for instance) or else it must occur at night when nobody is close by to disturb them. I approached the tank as stealthily as possible on some nights with a flashlight, hoping to catch the youngster in the act of nursing, but always the two would simply be swimming about slowly together or resting side by side on the floor of the tank. I left instructions with the night pumpmen and watchmen to keep an eye out for any sign of feeding activity, but to no avail.

Yet the baby was obviously being fed, for she continued to grow fairly rapidly and she soon became quite plump as well. Considerably more fearless than Cleo, the baby would readily allow herself to be fondled, and I delighted in lifting her partway out of the water by her tiny flippers. When I did this, she would often roll her small eyes upward so as to show the whites, and she seldom made any resistance on the occasions when I would remove her from the tank for weighing, although manatees, like dolphins and porpoises, are totally aquatic and never leave the water for any reason, so that removal from it, no matter how briefly, must be a most unnatural experience for these mammals.

The calf not only grew but was apparently browsing on algae as well, for her nose and lips were showing constant green stains. Finally, we noticed her nuzzling and apparently swallowing some of the algae that was growing on the wooden feeding ring (which we still used for Cleo since it kept particles of floating food from spreading all over the tank surface). This indicates that young manatees are evidently quite precocious, as she was still only just a little over a month old when she commenced to do this.

Then, on September 27, a remarkable coincidence occurred. I received a phone call from the Coral Gables Police Department stating that a young and apparently orphaned manatee had been observed that day swimming about the keel of one of the department's patrol boats, which lay tied to a dock in the Coral Gables Deep Waterway, about 5 miles from the Seaquarium. The corpse of a large manatee had been seen floating by

Young manatee under the keel.
Courtesy of Craig Phillips.

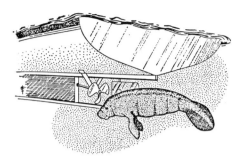

some time earlier, apparently killed by collision with a boat, and it appeared that this might have been the baby's mother.

Captain Gray and the truck were out making a call that afternoon, and experience has taught me to take advantage of any opportunity, if at all possible, without any delay. Recalling my successful capture by hand of the first orphaned manatee, I decided to repeat this event, if possible. I placed a large dipnet in the back of my car, and then rang up my wife on the phone. "Fanny," I said, "put on your swimsuit right away. We're going to catch another manatee!" "Oh, wonderful!" was the reply. "I'll be all ready!"

As we arrived at the dock I saw a ripple at the surface of the water by the stern of the boat. I had changed to my swimming trunks and was carrying the dipnet, and on boarding the boat, I saw the little sea cow disappear beneath the keel. Walking around, we spotted it as it appeared on the other side. This one looked the exact size of Cleo's baby, and appeared to be in good health, not showing the emaciated condition of the first little one in Hurricane Harbor. As it again came swimming leisurely toward the stern, I raised the dipnet above it to attempt to slip it over the manatee's head, but at that point it saw me and stopped swimming, lying close by the side of the boat with its head at the surface and its tail curved down beneath it.

In this position it would be difficult to net and we might lose it. On the other hand, it seemed quite unafraid and its flippers were within easy reach of my arms. Remembering the comparative simplicity with which I had secured the Hurricane Harbor specimen, I dropped down on my knees, reached over the rail, and grabbed it firmly by each flipper. Then, straightening my back, I prepared to haul it aboard with one continuous motion.

Somehow or other, the exact opposite happened. The manatee instantly turned a half-somersault and pulled me into the canal headfirst, without even a chance to call to Fanny, who stood some distance behind me. With a crash of foam I plunged downward into the dark water, still retaining my grip on the creature's wrists. He may have turned the tables on me, I remember thinking, but he's not going to get loose from me so long as I can hold my breath! (The fact that this obviously would not be forever did not occur to me at the time.) I was stubborn and determined, and I was going to take him back to the Seaquarium, and that was that.

After being pulled this way and that by the terrified little manatee, we both broke surface, which was lucky, since I was already beginning to choke on the water I had inadvertently swallowed during our descent. Twice he all but twisted out of my grasp, and I was actually surprised at how strong he was. Finally I managed to pull him against me and locked my arms around his chest, meanwhile shouting to Fanny for assistance. As she came swimming toward me, the manatee started making frantic swimming motions in my arms, alternately bending forward and then rapidly straightening his body. Each time he performed this latter maneuver, the back of his head hit me across the bridge of my nose. This was uncomfortable, and I was also becoming quite exhausted from treading water, though still close to the boat. Fanny reached my side in a moment, and with each of us holding on to a flipper, we managed to bring the baby into shallow water and drag him up on shore.

We were especially delighted to discover that he was a male. Now we had twin manatees! Now if only Cleo would adopt him also! The owners of the house behind the dock brought their station wagon up to the drive, and Fanny and I rode in the rear with the manatee back to the Seaquarium where we weighed him before placing him in the tank with the others. To my surprise, they were nearly identical in size, the female baby weighing 37 pounds and the male 41. On being placed in the tank, the little male began swimming about actively, and Cleo and her baby seemed more alert than usual, but other than that there was no visible sign of recognition on the part of any of them, being the inscrutable beasts that they are.

Next morning, both babies were resting on the bottom, one on either side of Cleo, and from then on both youngsters usually swam close together, either side by side or in tandem, occasionally making endless circles of the tank while Cleo dozed on the bottom. Within a few days it was apparent that Cleo had adopted the newcomer as her own, as he was noticeably plumper and looked well on the way to outgrowing his foster-sister. He was becoming quite active as well, although he never became quite so tame as the little female, who had been used to human handling from birth.

Still, we were unable to catch Cleo in the act of nursing either baby. This will always remain a mystery to me, as they were under observation most of the time and sooner or later one would have expected to obtain a glimpse of this process. For that matter, neither did we ever see her prod or nuzzle the babies as mammalian mothers customarily do, nor did she ever show the slightest objection (or any awareness of the fact, for that matter) when we removed either baby from the tank for measuring and weighing. In natural history books on the subject of Sirenians (manatees and dugongs), one almost invariably finds the statement: "They are said to clasp their young to their bosom as they rise out of the water to breathe." While I will not deny that this is a possibility, I have never seen any behavior of this sort during the time I observed Cleo, as well as another manatee mother with a baby at a Florida aquarium. However, it would be presumptuous to say that this never happens, since, for the same reason that I have never seen it, I could equally well assert that they do not nurse their young!

The fact is that much remains to be learned about the Sirenians, which are perhaps the most atypical of all aquatic mammals in that they are individualists and totally unlike any other creatures in the world. Lacking the amazing intelligence of dolphins, the aggressiveness of sea lions, and the playfulness of the seal and the otter, they nonetheless have a unique sweetness and charm that is entirely their own.

The two babies grew rapidly in the tank during the following month before I went on vacation. I had a great sense of pride in having been able to add another member to the family, as I have never heard of this having been done anywhere before. I left them for what was to be two weeks with considerable regret, as I didn't wish to miss the opportunity to make any additional observations that might contribute to general knowledge concerning the habits of manatees.

On returning from vacation late in October, I arrived at the Sea-quarium with a certain feeling of foreboding—almost a premonition—that something detrimental had happened to them during my absence. Nonetheless, I kept telling myself that I was just a chronic worrier and that my anxiety was simply due to my emotional involvement with their progress.

Unfortunately, my worries were only too well founded. All the manatees became sick soon after my departure, and the little female had become progressively thinner and had died two days before my return. Moreover, Cleo was going blind in one eye, a thing that should have tipped me off to the true nature of their condition. But anyhow it was too late. Cleo died the next day, and several days later the little male died too.

By then I had my suspicions, and I had the manatees autopsied by a local vet, who discovered the truth. During my absence from the Seaquarium and strictly against orders, one of the maintenance personnel had sprayed the area adjacent to the manatee tank with DDT and Chlordane in an effort to kill mosquitoes, and airborne oil droplets containing these deadly poisons had settled on the water surface. The chemicals were gradually absorbed by the manatees who could not tolerate them.

Cleo's body was frozen and shipped to the University of California for scientific study. Eventually we did obtain some more manatees, but the untimely death of our family remains one of the saddest events of my experience, as Cleo and the babies will always be, to me, irreplaceable.

My own first experience with a baby manatee followed in June 1965, the year after Craig Phillips's book was published. It was brought to Miami's Seaquarium by two young men who professed ignorance of Florida's strict conservation laws (and $500 fine) that protected the species at that time. The baby had been taken during an unsuccessful (and illegal) attempt to net its mother. The captors foolishly kept the offspring instead of immediately releasing him to return to his parent. They brought him to me for a quick sale and profit but instead stumbled into trouble for which they had not bargained. Accompanied by members of our collecting boat crew, they promptly were sent out to relocate the mother, but in vain. The damage was done, and now the mammal had to be cared for because he was far too young to be returned to the wild on his own. He was placed in a pool containing our adult male and female manatees, Romeo and Juliet, and through the Florida Department of Natural Resources we obtained the necessary permits to keep him.

Boxes of Pablum, cases of evaporated milk, hot water bottles, soaps, oils, vitamins, books, journals, weights and measures, and assorted paraphernalia heralded his arrival. The first chore was to mix a feeding formula that consisted of one can of evaporated milk thickened with baby cereal to which was added a teaspoon of cod liver oil. (R.C. Best and William E. Magnusson, Instituto Nacional de Pesquisas da Amazonia, Manaus, Brazil, reported in 1979 maximum digestibility and calf growth rates on powdered cow's milk.) Preliminary attempts with Craig's calf bucket apparatus were unsuccessful; the little fellow would shy away from the pail, and the contents spilled into the water. The problem of getting the entire unit under the water to him was solved by affixing the calf nipple to a hot water bottle. Now he could be chased about at least to the depth of arm's reach of the feeder. In no time he associated the bottle and nipple with food. Thereafter, when the hot water bottle was held in

During the 1960s Romeo and Juliet enjoyed the hide-tingling stimulus of the author's brush. Both Romeo and Juliet are still at Seaquarium, but Juliet bears the burden of grandparenthood and the author has retired. Only Romeo remains the passive Triton of his captive domain. Photo courtesy of Miami Seaquarium.

the pool he would go straight to it and consume every ounce. Some was lost into the water, spilling in milky clouds from both sides of his mouth. His constant hunger, coupled with the slight losses during feeding, encouraged me to double the formula and to substitute broad spectrum liquid vitamins for the cod liver oil. Now we shifted back to Craig's nursing pail, and this volume proved slightly more than enough for twice-a-day feedings; the overage prevented him from swallowing air at the end of the feeding.

The two adults in the pool got lettuce, cabbage, bananas, and bread crusts each afternoon. Soon the baby was observed nibbling at this roughage in addition to his private feedings. Of course, the reverse was true also. During feedings with the calf pail, the bull, in particular, would attempt to push the baby aside to get at the nipple. I permitted him to take it just once, whereupon he obtained such a firm grip on the nipple that he drained the entire formula and tore the nipple from the pail, to my embarrassment and to the total delight of guests who had crowded about to watch the tug of war.

The baby began to refuse the formula once and sometimes twice each day after twenty-two days of nursing. He continued to eat what appeared to be ever-increasing quantities of lettuce and other vegetation placed in the pool for the adults. His excrement became extremely hard at this time, so a few ounces of mineral oil were blended into his formula before the

Based on Craig Phillips's sketch, the author followed the identical procedure years later with another orphaned baby. Buckets of Pablum and milk provided adequate nourishment. Photo courtesy of Miami Seaquarium.

situation became serious. Two nursings with this additive seemed to solve the problem. From then on, we gave him formula once a day, and the adult vegetable diet was increased by one-half case of lettuce a day to include the baby.

Small, round white areas became evident on the skin of all three manatees. Their number and size increased rapidly, and they appeared particularly raw around the nostrils. We did not know the cause of this mottling, but the same condition had been recorded in years past as a self-limiting annoyance. Rather than take chances with the young animal, the water in the pool was converted from salt- to freshwater for twenty-four hours. Apparently this did the trick, as the infected areas on all three rapidly healed. This method had been successful once before in ridding the adult manatees and their artificial environment of a destructive marine ectoparasitic infestation of copepods.

By August 1965 the baby had lost all interest in the formula. With no information on his age, on weaning, or on just about anything else for that matter, we put aside the calf pail and increased the adult diet by still another half case of lettuce each day. The baby continued to thrive and grow.

During the years before this young manatee arrived, Romeo had been unsuccessful in mating attempts with Juliet. Perhaps it was coincidence, but the presence of the baby appeared to stimulate vigorous love play between the adults. Romeo even made many advances to the baby,

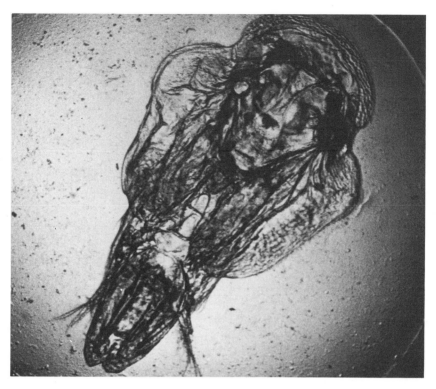

The microscopic copepod *Harpacticus pluex*, a parasite, infested the manatees' artificial environment before the baby arrived, causing potentially serious injury to Romeo and Juliet. Strong solutions of copper sulfate failed to destroy the pests, but a change from saltwater to fresh eliminated the problem. Photo courtesy of Miami Seaquarium.

clutching it in what most observers misinterpreted to be the legendary embrace. Finally, the adults were observed over a period of several days completing the act of copulation, and I hoped that in months to come we would be able to report a new arrival that would be of tremendous importance to the scientific community: the first manatee conceived and born in captivity. One day in November, however, when I made my early morning visit to the pool, I discovered the baby dead. Gordon Hubbell, veterinarian at the nearly Crandon Park Zoo, found in the autopsy that his intestinal tract was totally stopped up by large quantities of fibrous palm fronds that had been hand-fed him by the general public. The adults ceased mating after we removed the dead juvenile, and time proved that no new baby would be born to them.

Craig's Cleo and her baby had been lost through contact with residues of pesticides; now this baby, too, was the victim of human ignorance. Silently I have shared with him one of life's saddest experiences.

Seaquarium's Mermaid Rescue Squad

*I*n my years as director at Seaquarium in Miami, I saw missions of mercy involving staff personnel and marine creatures of every conceivable description become almost commonplace. The simple truth is that our animals are paramount in our lives, whether we are cooperating with scientists, arranging displays for the enjoyment and education of the public, or working with each other.

Our concern extends to wild creatures as well, from whales that strand themselves for unknown causes, to any life form unsettled or harmed, on purpose or by accident, by people. So often did this distress involve manatees that local newswriters dubbed the crew who answered these calls for help the "Mermaid Rescue Squad."

The author (in white shirt) bears a hand on a guide line as members of the Mermaid Rescue Squad guide a stretcher bearing an injured manatee into a special holding facility. The wounds were deep and rank with infection; she could not be saved. Photo courtesy of Miami Seaquarium.

This manatee's back was shredded by a boat propeller. Although extremely powerful swimmers, manatees cannot escape whirling blades. Few manatees throughout their Florida range do not bear grisly evidence of such encounters. Photo courtesy of Miami Seaquarium.

The 75-foot steel-hulled yacht, *Seaquarium*, was the hub of the squad's activities. Captain Charles Buie, his crew, and the staff veterinarian were on 24-hour emergency call. In years past every plea for assistance was checked for details and accuracy, and then the squad went into action. In recent years Florida's Department of Natural Resources created the Marine Patrol, a law enforcement division dedicated to upholding all coastal state legislation. In addition to apprehending everything from drug smugglers to lobster poachers, these officers are empowered by the U.S. National Marine Fisheries Service to act on their behalf as governing agency for both the Marine Mammal Protection Act of 1972 and the Endangered Species Act of 1973. Emergency calls to Seaquarium are now immediately referred to the Marine Patrol. If the Marine Patrol officer needs assistance, he or she will summon the squad to the scene.

Successful manatee rescues combine skill with good guesswork and luck. In 1968 the Mermaid Rescue Squad captured an adult sea cow that had been shot with a speargun. The veterinarian removed the spear and treated the wound successfully, and the animal was released in good condition. In another case, a severely bloated manatee was brought to Seaquarium completely unable to submerge, so that her back was blistered by the sun. Intubation and an abdominal puncture offered only temporary relief. Bloating recurred, and she was unable to eat. In spite of a month of intensive care, she died of unknown natural causes.

Another rescue began with a suspicious construction worker. For a time, no one suspected that the dead-end canal off the Miami River near

Few manatees in Florida waters have managed to avoid encounters with boat propellers. These victims did not survive. *Left,* photo courtesy of National Fish and Wildlife Laboratory. *Right,* photo courtesy of Daniel Odell, Ph.D.

the Miami International Airport had been selected by a huge female manatee for her private calving place. The area was as barren and bleak as any of the hundreds of other excavation sites throughout the state. All around, crushed oolite, the chalky white limestone Florida substrate dredged to create the waterway, reflected the blinding rays of the tropical sun. Heavy industrial equipment had bulldozed and dragged endless tons of oolite into a dam that isolated the canal from the river. The pond's sole water supply was through percolation from the shallow water table below. High banks protected its surface from disturbance even by the wind.

Periodically, something did disturb that milky mirror; workers noticed a large, grayish-brown object breaking the surface, and always very near, a second, much smaller one. In each mound, two small holes opened, then closed, before the mounds disappeared, leaving only concentric water rings expanding to shore. "Must be sea cows trapped in here," muttered one of the men, and he hurried to notify the Marine Patrol. Officers responding to the call found a mother and calf who soon

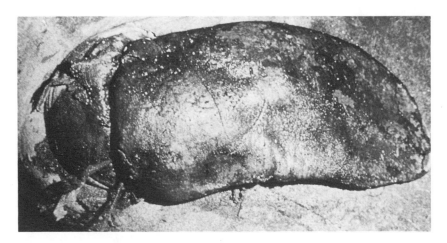

Thin, cutting nylon line apparently was tied to this animal's flipper on purpose, possibly to secure it to a boat. The rope broke and she escaped the immediate problem, only to die a lingering death. Complete cessation of blood circulation through the tournequeted limb caused it to rot, and she died of infection. (C-74-4/SWF-TM-7403-B; Female; 290 cm; November 11, 1974; Brevard County, Cocoa Beach.) Photo copyright 1974 by Sea World, Inc. All rights reserved. Reproduced by permission.

would starve to death in that barren pit. A slip might be cut through the dam, but there was no assurance that the female would take her calf through to the river. Seaquarium got a call to marshal the squad at the site at 0900 hours the following morning.

The crew arrived with their special equipment and in short order had the calf netted and safely ashore, but the huge female was a different story. With each set of the net she thrashed her way out. While that effort continued, marine mammologists from the Rosenstiel School weighed, measured, and took rectal temperatures of the calm baby. By 1700 hours the exhausted officers and crew decided to quit for the night. They would return the following day for another try. Since the calf apparently was newborn, they returned him to the pond and his mother for the night.

The following morning they again netted the baby with ease, and again the female thrashed her way out. The problem seemed to be that she always made good her escape in the deeper water offshore where the men were unable to gain purchase on the net or foothold on the unstable bottom. To lure her into shallow water, a soft line was secured around the baby's tail, and he was tethered in the water near shore like a pup on a leash. The dam knew the minute her offspring entered the water and

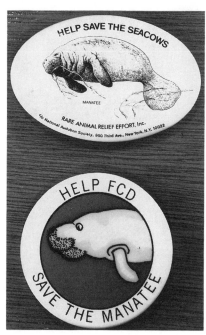

Window and bumper stickers are distributed throughout Florida and the United States as reminders of the plight of the state's and the nation's endangered manatees. Materials distributed by Central and Southern Florida Flood Control District, West Palm Beach, Florida.

immediately raced to his aid, right where the crew wanted her. She was secured in the net and swung across the oolite dam to the open river. The calf was carried by hand and the two were put into the water together. Only concentric water rings expanding to the opposite shore and diminishing up and down river indicated their presence.

One Mermaid Rescue Squad rescue, the saga of Sewer Sam, was portrayed on the "Undersea World of Jacques Cousteau" in an episode

Daniel Odell takes measurements, weight, and temperature. Data by Daniel Odell. The baby was constantly moistened to prevent his being dried out by the blistering sun. Photo courtesy of Miami Seaquarium.

Less than a week old, the manatee is carried to safety from the canal in which he and his dam soon would have starved to death. Photo courtesy of Miami Seaquarium.

The wary expressions on the faces of the men of the Mermaid Rescue Squad display their respect for the power of adult manatees. Photo courtesy of Miami Seaquarium.

With her baby as a lure, the huge female finally is ensnared in the net close to shore. No docile creature, she exerts the full force of her half-ton muscular body in a vain attempt to escape efforts on her behalf. Photo courtesy of Miami Seaquarium.

At last the reluctant female is in the bag, to be returned to the Miami River from which she had come seeking solitude to bear her calf. Photo courtesy of Miami Seaquarium.

Artie Melachi and Captain Buie guide the female manatee safely over the dam. The support pipes of the canvas stretcher bow under the load, but they will hold. Photo courtesy of Miami Seaquarium.

Officers of the Florida Department of Natural Resources help slide an emaciated Sewer Sam into a temporary infirmary until he recuperates. No marine mammal is maintained alone for long; they are kept among their own or with other compatible species, and Sam soon joined the resident manatees for the balance of his Seaquarium stay. Photo courtesy of Miami Seaquarium.

called "The Forgotten Mermaids." Sam was a 1,200-pound manatee that took a wrong turn in the North Miami labyrinth of canals and ended up wedged in a concrete drain culvert 33 inches across. He might have died there had not his bulk effectively dammed heavy rain runoff. A workman who crawled into the pipe to trace the cause of the blockage was surprised to find the exhausted beast squinting back at him in the damp dark tunnel. The press dubbed the manatee Sewer Sam, and the squad rallied to this new challenge. Poor Sam, weakened from starvation, was rescued from the culvert with no more than a bad bruise on the top of his nose. He was brought to Seaquarium, treated and placed in the exhibit with our resident male and female to be fattened up and to regain his strength before being returned to the wild.

Sam's story might have ended there had not his plight and subsequent rescue been brought to the attention of Captain Jacques Cousteau. Cousteau and his son, Philippe, had been working during the autumn in the St. Johns River basin on "The Forgotten Mermaids." As winter's chill creeps southward the manatee populations on Florida's northwest coast migrate from the Gulf of Mexico to Crystal River, a thermal refuge where the water temperature seldom varies from a constant 74° F. Even here their sanctuary is in a precarious state. Cousteau and his team found civilization's trademarks everywhere, from the Gulf of Mexico to the springs themselves. By November, hordes of campers and tourists descend upon the area, and the manatee congregation must share this diminishing wilderness with them. Usually by March, Gulf waters have warmed sufficiently for the animals to again go their separate ways; they are not gregarious and normally are seen alone or in a mother and calf pair.

Cousteau's team left the area and flew south to Miami, drawn by the tale of Sewer Sam, who had been recuperating in the small Seaquarium display tank for more than a year. Only the distinctive white scar on his nose remained as evidence of his trauma. He was ready to return to his aquatic domain and, with his prodigous appetite for endless cases of fresh lettuce, Seaquarium officials were ready as well.

Cousteau had conceived a plan to return Sam to freedom, not in the metropolitan Miami area but in the warm waters of Crystal River 600 miles away. Manatees apparently require no reconditioning before being returned from a captive to a wild environment, unlike big cats or great apes. They need only one thing: plenty of food. Barring intervention by their only existing hazard, humans, a freed manatee will simply eat its way happily into the sunset. While the logistics of Sam's long move were

Philippe and Captain Jacques Cousteau reaffirm plans for the last half-mile of Sam's journey to the spring. Under the watchful eye of the area Department of Natural Resources officer, the hydrocrane will lower the watertight box into the canal. Photo by the author.

being plotted in Miami, Cousteau's men prepared for Sam's arrival. They constructed a sturdy observation raft in a separate spring one-half mile from the main waterway and connected to it by a reasonably deep clear stream. The spring, lush with aquatic plant growth, was warm, and the clear water was continually replaced by an abundant flow from underground. Philippe had selected a secluded natural amphitheater within which Sam would strut his hour upon the cinematographers' stage. With the stage set, Sam began his journey to freedom. Staff veterinarian Jesse White was with the squad when Sam was rescued and

The inflatable, shallow-draft, highly maneuverable Zodiac is the crew's workhorse. It purrs around a bend in a stream within the cypress forest that seals out the encroaching world. Photo by the author.

had cared for him ever since. Throughout the trip he would be at Sam's side. I was there, too, inexpertly photographing everything and assisting wherever possible.

Finally, necessary state permits for Sam's move were obtained; a crane, truck, and personnel were ready, and the chartered DC3 was standing by at the airport. The camera crew, Philippe, and Captain Cousteau were on the scene and filming. Water had been drained from the manatee tank, and the specially constructed, heavily padded shipping box was in place on the bottom on its side. Sam, all 1,200 pounds of him, was to be rolled carefully into the box, which would be turned upright and snatched out of the tank and onto the waiting truck by the crane, and off we all would go. Everything any of us could think of had been arranged and was in complete readiness, except Sam. He rolled over and over, slapped his immense broad tail and thrashed this way and that, bowling men over like tenpins. When directly engaged with the "Undersea World of Jacques Cousteau," the men in the tank contained their epithets out of respect for the cameras and microphones—or they may have been drowned out by shouts of encouragement, first for the men, then for Sam, from the chorus of sidewalk superintendents.

Finally Sam was snug within the padded box, and amid a cacophony of English and French I pitched my valise on the flatbed and pulled myself aboard. Carefully, we drove to the highway and on to the airport with our precious cargo. Cousteau's camera crew followed by car, filming from behind, passed us on the right and then on the left, pulled ahead to film from the front, and sped on to set up and await Sam's arrival on the runway next to the aircraft. A forklift transferred the box from truck to plane with Doc White and me and Philippe always at Sam's side. Philippe filmed onboard, and the other camera crew and Captain Cousteau boarded a smaller aircraft to follow and film the DC3 from every possible angle on our flight to Crystal River. They landed ahead of us and set up on the ground to film our landing. Waved off, we came around again for one last take. The DC3, bearing so light a load, responded smartly to the wave off. Although I had some trouble keeping down the snacks I had eaten during the two-hour flight, Sam remained apparently undistressed. We touched down gently, rolled to a stop, and unloaded our charge onto another waiting truck for the short drive to the waterway leading to Sam's temporary new home. A crane lifted the box into the water, and it was then towed upstream to the spring impoundment by the outboard-powered Zodiac. Philippe and one of the divers guided the box, now a floating barge, into the water from astern, while Doc and I joined the captain and his crew manning the outboard in the Zodiac.

At each bend in the stream we ran head-on into the omnipresent camera, and I very professionally stared intently in any direction except toward the lens. At Sam's private spring, we maneuvered the Zodiac and towed box through the gap in the corral and tied up to the raft. Several men drove long stakes into the bottom, completing the enclosure behind us. The moment we all had worked for was close at hand. Phillipe applied his weight to one corner of the box, just enough to permit entrance of the cool spring water at a very slow rate in order to prevent temperature shock. Soon the box was filled, and the soft foam pads floated out from under the manatee. The box was completely on its side, and true to the pace he had set earlier in Miami, Sam would not budge. We began to watch his nostrils to see if he would take a tell-tale breath and indicate he was still alive. He did, and at last, with a flick of his tail, he propelled himself into the spring and lazily began to survey his new domain. "Voila,

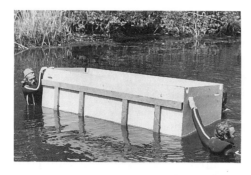

Sewer Sam's royal barge is floated into the secluded spring he will call home for a two-week readjustment period. Cautiously, Sam slips past the diver into the crystalline water. Photos by the author.

Sammy, Sammy!" shouted the captain, a broad grin of relief and personal satisfaction on his face.

Our concern at this point was Sam's insatiable appetite. Would he eat the hydrilla weed that grows on the bottom throughout this entire watershed area? He had been given no food for twenty-four hours before shipment and now by all sea cow standards should have been ravenous, but he ignored the luxuriant aquatic growth and continued to inspect his environment. We grew anxious; in order to survive Sam had to eat. Just in case a bit of feeding stimulus might be required, I had carried along a plastic bag of the bread crusts he liked. Philippe had some too, but we first tossed several slices of mine out toward Sam. They sank to the bottom to be fought over by myriads of fishes and blue crabs. Philippe placed one of his large pieces just in front of Sam's nose as he approached the surface for a breath of air. His nostrils opened and closed, and he manipulated the crusty loaf into his mouth with his bristly lips.

Great cheers from Cousteau's men resounded through the wilderness as Sam consumed crust after crust of French bread. Thus triggered, the feeding machine reverted to form and set to work on the aquatic vegetation. Captain Cousteau set the first watch; Sam would not be alone for so much as a minute until he finally made his way to complete freedom. We boarded the Zodiac and made for our own quarters for the night.

In the morning we hurried back to the site, where the watch reported all had been normal throughout the night. We sat on the edge of the raft and watched Sam resting peacefully on the bottom. Morning's chill drew wispy vapor breaths from the warm surface of the spring, illuminated by

Sam and friend spend endless hours at their game of hide-and-seek. Photo by
the author.

shafts of sunrise penetrating boughs draped with Spanish moss, and the
serenity of this primeval cathedral belied the "humania" beyond. Underwater cameras were loaded, and the men donned oxygen rebreathers and
slipped silently beneath the morning mist into the spring. Sam shied
away, nestling down among the hydrilla. The divers approached again,
and he responded by seeking another hiding place. Over and over the
gentle game of tag repeated itself and each cautious flight of beast from the
men provided the cinematographer with little more than identical views
of Sam's posterior. One of the men changed the pace by settling deep into
the hydrilla. No telltale exhaust bubbles escape from oxygen rebreathers.
We on the raft could see into the spring, but to an underwater viewer, the
diver had disappeared. He was over here, Sam was there, both waiting. It
was Sam that broke first and seemed to search around for the diver. He
found him; the diver swam to another location among the weeds, whereupon Sam sought him again. The game went on for a very long time for so
unintelligent a beast as a manatee. Finally, Sam's attention turned to
breakfast, and the diver reboarded the raft. The hide-and-seek had been

an unanticipated turn of events for an animal with as smooth a brain as the manatee's, and Philippe and the captain were highly pleased to have caught this rare behavioral sequence on film.

We stayed close to our charge for the next few days and rapidly realized that he could not possibly have been in more kindly and concerned human hands. With great reluctance, we bade Sam, Philippe, and Captain Cousteau and their crew farewell and returned to our many other marine charges at Seaquarium. Back in the spring at Crystal River, within two weeks the corral stakes were removed. A pinger had been fastened around the base of Sam's tail by a material that would rot quickly in the water and drop away. He was to be tracked with a sonar receiver for as long as possible in his journeys through the waterways to freedom.

True to form, Sam proved a thoughtless and thankless subject and in the end had to be driven from the spring's haven to the hazards of the world. After several days and nights, he joined a small group of manatees and at last regained his freedom.

The pinger had dropped off after a few days, as planned, and although Sam bore a white scar on his nose that would forever identify him, he has never been seen or reported since.

Romeo, Juliet, and the Seaquarium Cast ≋

*R*omeo and Juliet have lived at Seaquarium for more than 30 years, and I have cared for them for most of that time. In 1974, when I became manager/curator, I decided that their 8,500-gallon environment, while adequate, was too limiting. In my files were copious notes and sketches for a greatly expanded manatee facility equipped with upper- and lower-level pools and a trickling waterfall beneath which one might stroll from the surface viewing area to the deeper end of the lower pool for underwater viewing. Pump and filters were to be housed out of sight within the structure that supported the smaller upper-level pool. The water was to be pumped from the lower pool through the filter to the upper pool, whence it would tumble back to the lower. I must admit that waterfalls of any elevation are nonexistent within the geographic range of the manatee in Florida. But a fall would have eye-appeal, would serve to aerate water recirculating within the system, and, through evaporation, would help reduce the too-warm water temperatures of south Florida's summer months. Our years of temperature records and the longevity of Romeo and Juliet at Seaquarium showed water temperature extremes of from 59° F to 89° F; this range, then, was tolerable for the Florida manatee (*Trichechus manatus latirostris*). The scientific literature had documented that manatees in the wild have died during cold snaps when low water temperatures held between 55° and 60° F, and the highest recorded over these years had not exceeded the 89° F listed for our own systems. This high had been recorded only for a single date, so while possibly it was uncomfortable for the aquatic mammals, it did not correlate with a single mortality among either wild or captive manatees. My notes include the comment that the system should achieve an ideal range of from no less than 60° to no more than 85° Fahrenheit.

For many years exactly how manatees breed had remained a mystery. Even the water depth that might be best for copulation was debated.

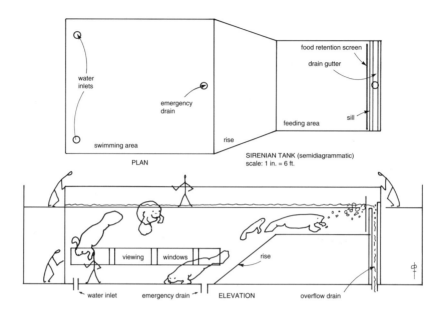

water inlets

emergency drain

swimming area

rise

food retention screen

drain gutter

feeding area

sill

PLAN

SIRENIAN TANK (semidiagrammatic)
scale: 1 in. = 6 ft.

viewing windows

rise

water inlet   emergency drain   ELEVATION   overflow drain

A manatee tank should consist of a swimming area with a depth at least equal to one and one-half times the length of a large animal and a shallow browsing area with a retaining screen for floating food, bottom water inlets at the deep far end, and a drain gutter at the shallow near end beyond the screen. The shallow browsing area is narrowed to produce enough water current to keep the vegetable matter against the screen until it is eaten. If the system must be closed, the water should be kept slightly brackish for all manatees except Amazonian freshwater species. A partial roof provides necessary shade; even so, the animals often grow enough algae on their backs to need regular scrubbing. Changing salinity helps to offset this problem, but a practical solution was devised at Seaquarium: placing several large gray mullet (*Mugil cephalus*) in with the manatees. They kept not only the backs of the manatees reasonably free of algae but the sides and floor of the tank as well.
Courtesy of Craig Phillips.

"They mate while in a vertical position and therefore depths of less than 10 feet will not do." "No, the position is horizontal so a 3-foot depth will suffice." "In fact, they have been observed close ashore, even partially emerged from the water against the bank." My tank design included a 3-foot depth beneath the waterfall dropping away to not less than 15 feet at the far end drain.

Water systems were to be changeable from fresh to salt to simulate the range of manatee migrations. Ectoparasitic infestations would be eliminated from both the animals and the total captive environment by alternating salt water to fresh (or vice versa), a natural control that occurs through their wanderings from the sea to rivers.

Fresh water was provided for drinking through a nuzzle-nozzle, a simple device that delivered water when the manatee depressed the trigger plate with its bristly snout. This simple bit of conditioning is handled easily by even so unintelligent a creature and conserves fresh drinking water provided from the city supply. Appropriate landscaping was to have completed the artificial environment, but the nation in the mid-1970s was emerging from the financial trauma of recession, and none of these plans could possibly become reality for several years.

The only on-hand facility suitable for Romeo and Juliet was the Celebrity Pool—160,000 gallons, depth 14 feet, diameter 40 feet, with large glass underwater windows around about 300° of its circumference. A water turnover rate of four times per day at a filtration rate of 24,000 gallons per hour is more than adequate to handle many more than two sea cows. This pool had been the home of our young killer whale (*Orcinus orca*), recently moved to his own new facility, and now was the home of two Pacific whitesided dolphins (*Lagenorhynchus obliquidens*). A single seawater chilling unit maintained the water temperature between 64° and 68° F, identical to the killer whale's environment. The solution seemed simple: move the Pacific whitesided dolphins in with the *orca* and place the manatees in the Celebrity Pool; its chiller could then be moved on line with those controlling the new whale facility as a back-up safety unit. Moving the dolphins there might seem parallel to casting Christians to the lions because they are part of the food chain of *orcas* in the wild. However, all known needs of the whale were provided for, and there seemed little reason to believe he would have cause to hunt. The dolphins were placed in the back section of the whale facility, separated from the whale by a wall in which there was an opening blocked by a heavy wooden bulkhead. In time the bulkhead was replaced by a heavy chain link gate. The whale and the dolphins, who had sensed each other's presence from the first moment, at this point could see each other as well. In time there seemed to be no fright pattern evidenced by the dolphins (and certainly none by the *orca*), so the gate was removed. Eventually, the dolphins swam into the large pool area and have coexisted peaceably with the killer whale ever since.

In December 1974 we were ready to move Romeo and Juliet to their new quarters. They would be joined by another adult female and her

Absolutely rotund, Romeo's great bulk is so well adapted to his aquatic environment that he and other members of our herd never fail to amaze viewers with their agility and grace. Asleep on the bottom they seldom elicit more than an "ugh," but soon one or more rises to the occasion (and to the surface for a breath of air) and performs a repertoire of pirouettes. Photo courtesy of Miami Seaquarium.

yearling female calf rescued by the Marine Patrol and the Seaquarium rescue squad after the female had been seriously injured by a boat propeller. She was almost completely healed by this time, and she and her calf would be much better off with others of their own kind rather than isolated in an infirmary tank. The presence of a juvenile several years before had stimulated sex play between Romeo and Juliet; with luck, this might again prove true either with Juliet or the new adult female, thus doubling the chances for conception. The move also gave us a unique chance to tape consecutive sequences of manatee communication.

Arthur Myrberg, a professor in the Department of Biology and Living

The dam and her approximately year-and-a-half-old female calf survey their new Celebrity Pool domain and their new companions, Romeo and Juliet. The scruffy appearance of both animals is a normal sloughing of skin that occurs periodically in a marine environment. Photo courtesy of Miami Seaquarium.

Resources of the Rosenstiel School of Marine and Atmospheric Science at the University of Miami, devised the step-by-step animal transfer plan that would best allow him and his staff to record communication and at the same time observe and tape behavior. Dam and calf communication norms were recorded in the infirmary tank for a two-hour period; Romeo and Juliet's norms were taped during this same time frame in their small tank. Romeo was moved to the Celebrity Pool, and data were recorded on him alone for two hours. Then Juliet was moved in with Romeo, and the two were observed and recorded for two hours. Finally, the sequence was repeated with the dam and her calf, then with all four in the Celebrity Pool together. After six or seven hours, Myrberg and his crew, exhausted, hoarse, and happy, were surrounded by reel after reel of invaluable data. "How long will it take to analyze what you've got?" I asked, completely naive about such matters and ready for answers ranging anywhere from a day or two to certainly no more than a couple of weeks. "Well, we should be able to get some computer time next year and have a printout a couple of months after that, then analyze, and perhaps have a rough draft in two years or so." The results are in fact yet to come in. The patience of dedicated research investigators is phenomenal.

Water clarity within the Celebrity Pool was excellent, and the underwater viewing windows presented an unlimited view of our four-manatee

Settled in her new home, beautiful, placid Juliet aroused great concern. The underwater viewing windows gave a first glimpse of the obviously distended vaginal area. Photo courtesy of Miami Seaquarium.

herd. An informal constant watch was maintained on the animals; for one thing, many questions about copulation remained. That Juliet was not herself became all too clear. The plump loveliness of her fusiform body was distorted by a swollen vaginal area. Perhaps she had injured herself internally during the move to the Celebrity Pool, in spite of every precaution. The possibility did exist that she might be pregnant. Her appetite was reaching herculean proportions, and the breasts beneath her forelimbs were more obvious than I had ever seen them. By January I was convinced that at some future date, barring a miscarriage, there would be a birth. The date was unpredictable because Sirenian gestation periods were a matter of speculation, and literature estimates ranged from 152 to 400 days. Our senior pumpman had noted sex play between Romeo and Juliet that past February but had not recorded penetration. All employees had been requested to note mating attempts, should they occur, after the produce diet had been augmented with 10 pounds of horse chow pellets per animal per day in an effort to increase calcium and phosphorus levels in their diet. Again, all employees were asked to keep watch. Daily I made numerous trips to the tank and for four months observed the swollen area enlarge and axillary teats swell until the dark grey-brown at their tip turned pink. Surely the time was near. At least one reference stated that a cow had stopped eating a day or two before birthing; Juliet's appetite continued to be prodigious.

At approximately 10:48 A.M. on Saturday, May 3, 1975, Juliet surprised and delighted the world by giving birth to a normal, healthy female. The

During the first quarter-hour of her life, Juliet's calf was assisted to the surface to breathe. More often than not, she rode on her mother's back, and she always maintained physical contact at least with her snout, pectoral flipper, or tail. Tiny hairs evenly spaced over her body were evidence of her mammalian heritage. A roll of tissue encircled the juncture of body and tail like baby fat. It took weeks for the fetal folds in her tail to straighten out to a smoothly rounded configuration. Photo courtesy of Miami Seaquarium.

joyous news reached me at home by telephone. "Is it all right, breathing, appear normal?" My mind raced over endless questions whose answers might be learned this exciting day. "Seems normal as far as we can tell," came the reply. "Did anyone witness the birth?" "No one on our staff, just one tourist who was there taking snapshots but we can't find him." "Keep on paging him over the public address system. We need those photographs." The tourist never was located. "Get our own photographer down there at once and tell him to shoot everything from every possible angle. How's Juliet? What is Romeo doing? The other two? What about the placenta? Get a diver down there and recover the placenta and have it stored under refrigeration until Doc arrives. Call in Doc right away. Notes, who is taking notes? Place employees topside and at the underwater viewing windows and have them jot down everything they see. Except for the diver recovering the placenta, no one is to enter the water unless the baby is endangered in some way. The list, the list, telephone everyone on the list. I'm on my way over!"

The list had been prepared at least two months before and included the telephone numbers of scientists from the Marine Lab, our staff veterinarian, Seaquarium management personnel, and our public relations firm. I especially wanted our public relations people there to consult with all of the others and get facts to the media without delay. During the twenty minutes that it took my wife, children, and me to reach Seaquarium and the Celebrity Pool, several employees recorded the baby's activities. They watched as Juliet, Romeo, and the other female adult pushed the baby to the surface to breathe. Juliet moved very slowly (one trainer noted that she seemed exhausted), accompanied for a time by the other female whose older calf did not approach the baby at all. Juliet nudged her offspring along with her bristly snout and several times manipulated it onto her back. In this position it appeared at rest and only raised its head a trifle in order to take another breath of air. The other female left her calf periodically and approached Juliet, stayed with her for a few minutes, and then returned to her own. Within fifteen minutes the baby was swimming on its own with little encouragement from the other manatees. Rarely did she lose complete contact with her mother; there always was some part of her touching.

At poolside, my family and I were greeted by laughter, smiling faces, everyone talking at once. I tried to retain my curatorial composure, but it fractured time and again as we shook hands all around. I passed out cigars and happily accepted slaps on the back and "Congratulations, Dad!" in spite of my protestations of innocence. The baby was the homeliest, funniest looking, most beautiful little creature I have ever seen. She represented something that had not happened before in the course of recorded history. Most of the questions regarding breeding still remained unanswered, but all facets of a manatee's life history would be revealed to us over the coming twenty, thirty, perhaps more years. This was just the beginning.

During the balance of her first day of life I became anxious for the welfare of the baby. Struggle as she might, nuzzling above and below, up and down the length of Juliet, she was unable to locate either nipple. Each time she neared the base of Juliet's flipper a cheer arose from the crowd, and her nuzzling quickened to a frantic pace. Everyone's disappointment was audible each time she missed the life-sustaining breast. The search would end, and for a brief while she would assume a rest position alongside or atop her dam; then the frantic search resumed once again. No one could guess how long such behavior could persist without jeopardizing the baby's chance for life. We were determined not to alter the course of nature unless it became absolutely necessary through Juliet's

Less than one hour old, the baby seemed bewildered by the transition from the saline environment of the womb to that of the sea. Photo courtesy of Miami Seaquarium.

refusal to nurse her offspring or its inability to locate a breast. We also agreed that we would attempt nothing in the way of assistance until after the second day, an extremely difficult decision. Among lower life forms mating produces an abundance of offspring, and no more than a few need survive to perpetuate the species. Higher forms, particularly mammals, bear few offspring. *Trichechus* species, bearing perhaps no more than one every several years, is an extreme case. Here nature provides parental care to improve survival odds. If we were to learn anything at all, nature had to take its course, and we would only step in to assist if nature failed. A 24-hour watch was set, and we left for the night. The following morning the watches' log bore the notation: "7:15 P.M., baby nursing."

By 10:00 A.M. of the second day, another hazard faced the 24-hour-old baby. There seemed to be excessive vocalization among the manatees, and Romeo began displaying what appeared to be aggressive behavior toward his daughter. Four times he clutched the calf with his flippers and lay on top of her on the bottom of the pool. Whether or not he intended harm was unclear, but during one of these episodes he held the baby with his right flipper and hit it continually with the left, almost in a spanking

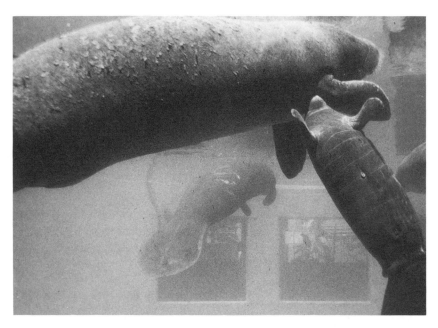

Wrinkly Lorelei nurses contentedly at just a few days of age. Note the bulge near Juliet's vent; it offered the first clue that she was pregnant. Photo courtesy of Miami Seaquarium.

manner. Juliet interceded the first few times, and thereafter her baby managed to free herself. Additional attempts by Romeo to clutch her calf were thwarted by Juliet. She fended him off with tail, flipper, or a sound thump on the head. The baby repeatedly gained a vantage point on top of Juliet's back just behind the head. Undaunted, Romeo succeeded in dislodging the infant but was prevented from grasping it by its own maneuvers and by aggressive moves by Juliet. Vocalization between the beasts was quite audible to the naked human ear during the fracas, from which the other adult female and her calf remained aloof. After two and one-half hours, enough was enough for us. Rather than chance injury or worse, we lured Romeo with lettuce and apple wedges into the satellite pool and closed the steel grill gate. There he would be isolated for a few days while I pondered certain literature that described diligent paternal care among manatees.

Soon both mothers obligingly lifted a pectoral flipper as their respective babies nuzzled for a nipple and suckled their fill. Later they would nurse from either female, or both from one, at will. The larger calf not only

Diver Alex Edlin holds Lorelei for her initial weigh-in. By the end of the first year she will prove too large for him to lift. Photo courtesy of Miami Seaquarium.

had nursed but had eaten produce as well from her first day in our care. I turned to the experiences of others for some idea of when we might expect the new baby to start consuming lettuce; the shortest time span of one of the only two previously recorded babies was thirty-eight days, and the other, four or five months. Juliet's baby ate lettuce at eleven days. I went to the Celebrity Pool for the usual herd feeding at 5:00 P.M. on May 14 and was amazed to see the infant clutching a lettuce leaf between the tips of her stubby flippers and inexpertly manipulating it into her mouth. From that point on, she consumed more each day and soon was competing with the adults for her share. When she had avoided chance injury or problems for her first month of life and had grown at a highly visible rate, we decided to take accurate weight and measurements. This necessitated draining the entire pool. She weighed 76 pounds and was 49 inches long. By her first birthday she weighed almost 200 pounds and was 5½ feet long.

This manatee deserved a name befitting her place in history. From the first day it was "baby this" or "little girl that" or "sea calf." We held a state-wide contest to find a proper name and to raise awareness of manatees as an endangered species; each entry submitted had to be accompanied by the reason for selection of that name, in fifty words or less. Grand prizes stimulated unprecedented participation, and soon my office was filled

A letter from Dr. D. Dekker of the Amsterdam Zoo announced the birth on August 8, 1977, of a West Indian manatee. Earlier correspondence had requested preparturition data and photographs of our pregnant Juliet. Note the sparse coat of hair over the bodies of both dam and calf. Photo courtesy of Natura Artis Magistra, Amsterdam, Holland.

with cards and letters. Most rewarding were the entries submitted and signed by entire school classes. It was apparent that teachers had taken advantage of the theme to educate children on the plight of the sea cow, lessons we prayed they would never forget.

Legend says that along the river Rhine, between the cities of Mainz and Koblenz, hidden somewhere on the 430-foot cliffs, are mysterious, beautiful, but wicked sirens who lure boaters and their crafts to death and destruction upon the rocks. They are the Lorelei; and so we named Romeo and Juliet's baby.

Two years after Lorelei's birth the August 8, 1977, birth of a male West Indian manatee was confirmed by D. Dekker of Artis, the Amsterdam Zoological Gardens, Netherlands. The sire, named Joop, had been taken in Surinam and arrived at the zoo in October 1966; his length today has remained the 8 feet 9 inches that he measured at that time. The dam, Mary, had been captured in Guyana and was introduced into the tank with the adult male in September 1972. In the years that followed she grew from 8½ feet to 9 feet. Sexual behavior first was noted between the two during the first week of August 1976. The male attempted to grasp the female with his flippers and at the same time evagination of the sexual organ was observed. Swelling of the female's genitalia was evident for about two

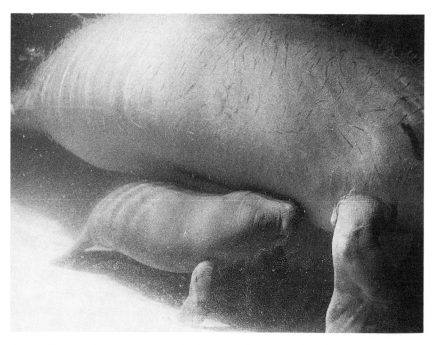

Amsterdam's infant manatee, only the second conceived and born in captivity, approaches its dam's pectoral nipple to nurse. Photo courtesy of Natura Artis Magistra, Amsterdam, Holland.

weeks. Intromission was not observed, however, and the episode was forgotten.

During 1977 changes in the female indicated that pregnancy was a possibility. She developed a huge appetite and consumed food so quickly that the male was unable to obtain his share of their daily ration of 110 pounds of lettuce and endive. He became conspicuously thinner while she became fat and rotund. To maintain the bull's health the two were separated; thereafter, he quickly regained weight. In addition to the female's increase in body circumference, during the month of May a distinct swelling appeared in the area of the genital pore. This persisted, and in time observers noted periodic undulating movements from the umbilicus to the tail. The movements continued through July. The abdominal thickness had moved toward the tail.

Again, the actual birth was not witnessed, but the little male apparently was lively and was described as beautifully round, a perfect miniature of his colossal dam. He stayed very close to her but surfaced more frequently to breathe than she did. During periods of rest he surfaced

Romeo and Lorelei indulge in courtship play. Ariel somewhat excitedly enters the courtship and apparently becomes a willing student of Romeo's advances. Neither youngster proved to be impregnated. Photos by the author.

every one to two minutes. Respiration intervals shortened to fifteen to thirty seconds during swimming exercise. During his first week, intervals lengthened to three or four minutes. The little male nursed successfully, and it was noted that in the beginning, if he suckled one nipple too much, his dam moved him to the other side with her pectorals. The female was highly protective of her offspring, and any imagined threat resulted in immediate response on her part, including manipulation of him with her flippers in order to position herself between him and the threat.

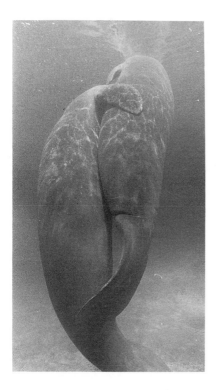

When the calf was two weeks old, the barrier separating the two from the bull was removed, and the three reunited without incident. Sire and dam quietly shared their daily ration. The baby manipulated and nibbled at this from the very first day but during the first two months was not observed actually consuming any of the produce.

At his birth on August 8 the manatee was estimated to be less than 3 feet 3 inches long. On August 24, his length was measured at 3 feet 4 inches; September 9, 3 feet 7 inches and 61.6 pounds; September 19, 3 feet 11½ inches and 68.2 pounds; and last reported on October 6, 4 feet 6 inches and 101 pounds. This would seem to reflect a rather healthy and rapid early growth. He was named Lamantinus. His parents, Joop and Mary, were doing fine in 1992. Lamantinus, however, was sent to Antwerp Zoo in 1981, where he died three years later. Mary's second baby, a female, was stillborn in 1987. The third, a male, was born in 1989 and is at Burgers Bush at Arnheim.

Seaquarium's three-year-old female calf, Ariel, first mated with Romeo in 1976. In 1979 her dam, Amanda, and Juliet both were suspected of being pregnant, each showing early signs noted for Juliet and the Artis

Estimates of age of sexual maturity of *T. manatus* recorded in the literature range from four to eight years. Our precocious calf, Ariel (brought in with her propeller-injured dam, Amanda), was observed mating with Romeo on June 8, 1976, at age three. She accepted him three times; during each, she remained in a horizontal position at the surface with Romeo on his back beneath grasping her with his flippers. She did not conceive. Photo courtesy of Miami Seaquarium.

female. Lorelei, like Ariel, engaged in early sex play as captured in the accompanying series of photographs. However, initial signs of vaginal swelling in the two adult females now are recognized as indicating oestrus, at least in Amanda's case. Juliet was another matter. At 2:30 A.M., August 3, 1980, she gave birth to her second female calf. With confidence gained from our first experience, we weighed and measured the newborn immediately; 72 pounds and 46½ inches. She was huge, yet she fell into place on the weight and length curves established for wild manatees. Romeo again was banished to the satellite pool, and Ariel and Lorelei, who had found the abundance of fresh milk in Juliet before the baby was born, were also separated from the adult females to ensure a sufficient supply.

There occurred on August 11, 1980, a small disaster that would lead to an event of immense importance to studies of Sirenian husbandry. I received a telephone call from members of the International Aquanaut Foundation (IAF) informing me of a very small manatee found bumping about the rocks at Hillsborough Beach by three young surfers. Governmental agencies let IAF bring the baby to Seaquarium after a full morning's search had failed to locate any other sea cows in the entire area. The youngster apparently had been orphaned, and in that busy water-traffic area one might surmise that a speeding boat had killed the mother. The

Measurements of Lorelei (in inches)

	6/6/75	7/27/75	8/15/75	10/17/75	11/25/75	2/13/76	6/18/76	5/13/77
Nose to tail	48.43	50.00	54.33	55.12	59.06	62.20	66.93	71.26
Nose to umbilicus	19.69	21.50	21.26	21.65	21.65	23.62	24.80	24.80
Nose to genital slit	29.53	30.98	33.07	34.65	35.43	37.40	40.55	43.31
Nose to anus	31.89	34.49	35.83	37.79	38.19	41.34	44.88	47.64
Fluke length	13.39	15.51	14.96	16.54	—	—	18.50	21.65
Fluke width	12.60	13.50	14.57	15.16	—	15.75	17.72	19.69
Flipper								
Anterior origin to tip	8.66	8.50	8.66	8.66	—	—	10.24	—
Axilla to tip	7.87	9.02	9.45	9.45	—	—	9.84	—
Width	3.15	3.27	3.54	3.54	—	—	4.33	—
Girth, axilla	25.98	—	30.31	29.53	31.10	—	38.98	40.55
Girth, umbilicus	30.70	—	36.22	—	40.16	—	48.82	50.00
Girth, anus	20.87	—	28.74	27.56	29.53	—	30.31	—
Tail stock	—	—	20.87	21.65	—	—	25.98	—
Weight (in pounds)	76	—	75	125.5	137	173	218	242

members of IAF halved rescue time by bringing the baby to us, saving precious hours of travel time by Seaquarium's rescue crew. Upon arrival the manatee was checked out throughly by veterinarian Jesse White, who found it to be a male suffering abrasions on his nose and back from the rocks. He was extremely weak and showed signs of dehydration and malnutrition. His weight and length were remarkably parallel to those of Juliet's new calf (named Alexandra as a result of another "name the baby" contest held by an interested local newspaper). We had faced this situation before and turned to the task at hand with little hope.

We placed the orphaned male baby in the pool with Amanda, Juliet, and her Alexandra. The trainers and Doc prepared for around-the-clock feedings, but dissatisfied with past formulas, Doc telephoned others in the field for possible alternatives. We tried Sea World's formula based on work with baby walruses. Far too frightened of the new unnatural surroundings, the male refused all attempts to nurse from a bottle, so day and night a tube was eased into his stomach and the formula pumped in. Thereafter, for days on end, employees took turns with the baby in the water, touching, caressing, trying to help him overcome his fear of humans, as well as of the other members of the manatee herd.

Our one hope was that in time the baby might accept Juliet as a surrogate mother, but each time she drifted by nursing her own baby, the terrified male thrashed away. The entire episode was heartbreaking. Many times we noted that when Juliet passed close to him she actually lifted her near pectoral flipper offering the life-giving breast. We all saw this time and again, and there was no doubt in any observer's mind that she was doing exactly that, even with Alexandra nursing contently on the opposite side.

Slowly, surely, the orphan's wrinkled concave midriff began to fill out, but having been through these traumatic experiences before, none of us allowed ourselves to hope. August passed, and the first two weeks of September, and a second weighing proved that he had gained a bit in weight and grown a few inches in overall length.

The price of lettuce, cabbage, and assorted greens that comprised our growing herd's normal diet was getting out of hand. Other member institutions of the American Association of Zoological Parks and Aquariums used commercially available hydroponic units to grow dense mats of various grasses for food. With such units in operation, the current costs, averaging $2,400 per month, could be reduced by as much as two-thirds. The equipment was obtained and put into operation. Optimum growth

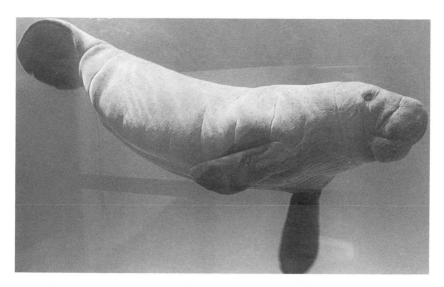

Alexandra strikes out on her own within the safe confines of her artificial environment. In the wild, instinct and learned fear would temper such boldness. Photo courtesy of Miami Seaquarium.

Amanda, identified by four propeller scars, and Juliet's Alexandra become acquainted during her first day of life. Bottlenosed dolphin social behavior provides a dam and infant with an "auntie," an adult female or male that assists with the baby. No such arrangement is documented for manatees, and the photograph may depict no more than mutual curiosity. Photo courtesy of Miami Seaquarium.

Alexandra and Jean-Pierre nurse at any time, day or night, either singly or at the same time. Photo courtesy of Miami Seaquarium.

time for the mat of rye grass is seven days, and at the end of the week I watched through the underwater viewing windows as the first crop was introduced into the tank. We knew that the manatees would take time to accustom themselves to this new nutritious diet. They nibbled at it a bit but, as anticipated, preferred the usual fare. Alexandra, like Lorelei, had consumed increasing quantities of produce since about her third week of life. The male baby, however, still was being bottle-fed or, failing that, tubed. As other employees watched with me, the baby male manipulated a small portion of the grass into his mouth with his tiny pectoral flippers and bristly, still bruised snout. Perhaps there was a chance for survival after all. Day after day he consumed more and more, still not enough, however, to sustain life without the formula feedings as well.

Lowry Park Zoo's bronze "mermaids" symbolize the institution. Despite weighing over 1,000 pounds, the sculpture seems to float, balanced only on the baby's tail. Sculptor Tom Tischler intended to create a work that would leave viewers with a permanent affinity for the manatee. Photo courtesy of Lowry Park Zoo, Tampa, Florida.

On September 15, 1980, there occurred an event unparalleled in the brief history of captive husbandry of *Trichechus manatus*. We observed and photographed both babies firmly affixed to Juliet's teats. We had suspected the male of nursing because of his steady improvement. His bruises were healing nicely, and signs of malnutrition no longer were evident. Now the event was recorded on film. We discontinued formula nursing, and the following data comparing Alexandra with the male are positive evidence that special care and feeding no longer were necessary.

Alexandra	*Male Orphan*
August 3, 1980	August 11, 1980
72.5 lbs. (birth weight)	74 lbs.
46.5 in.	47.5 in.
September 15, 1980	September 15, 1980
96 lbs.	80 lbs.
52 in.	50 in.
October 16, 1980	October 16, 1980
141 lbs.	130 lbs.
55 in.	53 in.

During the data gathering, I asked Doc, "Now that he seems to have a good chance for survival, what are you going to call him?" "Jean-Pierre," he laughed. An employee nearby shouted something to the effect that that was a stupid name, but I cut him off. "He saved him, and by God, he can call him anything he wants!"

Jean-Pierre continues to prosper, as do Romeo, Juliet, Lorelei, Amanda, and her calf, Alexandra. In years to come there is little doubt that J. P. will assume the role of herd bull from the aging Romeo, introducing new genes, strength, and vitality into the herd. The relatively brief history of the Seaquarium colony has shown the age of puberty of the West Indian manatee is about seven and one-half years. Calving intervals within the herd ranged from fifteen to ninety-one months. The shortest intervals are displayed by Juliet, which one might predict because she (and the sire Romeo) has been longest in captivity. It might be optimistically deduced that the longer the females are maintained in a captive environment, the shorter the calving interval, at least to the minimum limit of fifteen months. This would dramatically increase annual reproduction efficiency within the captive herd.

In a birth sequence considered typical among aquatic mammals, the tail-first presentation increases survival chances by preventing drowning during a prolonged delivery. *Top*: the youngster is approximately two-thirds into its new world. *Bottom*: the dam rolls on her back, stretching the amniotic sac and freeing the youngster from the womb.

Top: a final twist separates the umbilicus in a burst of blood. *Bottom*: the babe is free and under scrutiny of its dam. Lorelei, the first conceived and born in captivity on May 3, 1975, gave birth to this healthy male specimen on June 28, 1984. The sire was Romeo; Juliet is the grandmother. Photo sequence by Ed Thompson, staff photographer, Miami Seaquarium.

Out of the Wilderness ❧

We should fight to prevent manatees from extinction for two practical reasons and one moral reason. The first practical reason is related to manatees being the world's only totally aquatic vegetarian mammals and to their voracious appetite for plants. The second practical reason concerns the suggestion that domesticating manatees can provide protein for human diets, particularly in areas of the world where protein is in short supply. The moral reason is that people are the Sirenians' major threat. We should in good conscience, if for no other reason, fight their extinction.

Noel D. Vietmeyer, professional associate in the Office of the Foreign Secretary, National Academy of Sciences, Washington, D.C., specializes in the uses of aquatic weeds and in how science can help developing countries. He cites the water hyacinth, *Eichhornia crassipes*, a single plant that is wreaking havoc throughout waterways in many parts of the world, and points to Guyana, which has used manatees successfully in the Botanic Gardens of Georgetown as aquatic vegetation control agents since 1885. By the late 1950s about a hundred manatees were performing this service, and some still are, years after being transported from Guyana's rivers to the canals. Almost a century of records show that the animals are remarkably nonselective about what they eat. They prefer succulent growth, but when this has been cropped or eliminated they will eat anything at all and will even browse the banks for plants. It is highly significient that they graze and efficiently convert to protein one of the most underutilized natural resources, aquatic plants.

This idea must be exciting to countries within the manatees' current range, and to other nations with environments that would support manatees to control aquatic weed infestations: Kenya, Sudan, Uganda, Bangladesh, India, Fiji, Indonesia, Malaysia, the Philippines, Sri Lanka, and the countries of Indochina. But enthusiasm for this seeming solution runs up against certain realities. Manatees are highly vulnerable to poaching and vandalism, particularly in the semiconfinement of narrow waterways. Irrigation drainage canals and other controlled water systems add the hazards of culverts, sluices, and locks. In open navigable waterways are the omnipresent boats and propellers. The manatees' almost nonexistent breeding record in confined areas of any type, as well as their slow rate of reproduction, have prevented them from being self-perpetuating. These hurdles must be faced, investigated, and overcome through research and educational programs. So little is known that opportunities for important research abound, especially in physiology, nutrition, biochemistry, pathology, breeding, and husbandry.

An article in a popular magazine in 1960 first directed the attention of the Central and Southern Florida Flood Control Board to the Guyana (then British Guyana) manatee projects. Since 1949, the board has directed Florida's comprehensive flood control and water conservation project. Eventually, a network of canals more than 2,000 miles long and 2,570 square miles of water storage areas and lakes will be incorporated into a system controlled by about 120 elaborate structures and pumping stations. The object of this costly and massive undertaking is to control the supply of fresh water and to prevent saltwater intrusion into the aquifer. When aquatic weeds threatened the system, the cost of controlling them by known chemical and mechanical means exceeded $500,000 a year in Florida alone. Quite possibly the only long-range answer lies in turning nature against herself through biological controls.

In 1964 the Flood Control governing board awarded a three-year contract to Florida Atlantic University in Boca Raton, Broward County, to study using the manatee to suppress aquatic and bank weed growth in essential inland waterways. Miami Seaquarium was contracted to provide the specimens for the study. The yacht *Seaquarium*, fully rigged and equipped for the unusual expedition, roamed the Intracoastal Waterway along Florida's lower east coast for two weeks. The ship anchored at various points along the coast, and the crew set out in small outboards to probe every inlet, canal, and creek between Fort Pierce and Miami. They finally found manatees in the Miami River, not far from the airport and a few miles from Seaquarium, which proved fortunate. Of the one male and four females taken, one female measured more than 11 feet in length and 9 feet around and weighed 2,170 pounds.

The five test animals were moved to the Broward County site where they proceeded to denude the quarter-mile section of canal of aquatic plants, first consuming those underwater. They pulled up plants such as cattail and spikeroot from the canal bottom and devoured their roots, as evidenced by rafts of plant debris on the water's surface. They fed steadily

Top: The two-week hunt for flood control district manatees ended in the Miami River. Bottom sediment boiled to the surface as each entangled giant was held with its head out of the water to prevent drowning. The action was repeated five times; each animal was safely brought to shore, then transferred to the collecting vessel for return to Seaquarium. *Side and bottom*: At the test site manatees are lowered carefully into the quarter-mile section of the canal fenced off for the initial stages of the operation. Note the reverse curve of the spine. This type of lift is hazardous to the animal and has been replaced with a heavy canvas pipe-supported stretcher designed to keep the beast flat, its weight evenly supported along the length of its body. Photos courtesy of Miami Seaquarium.

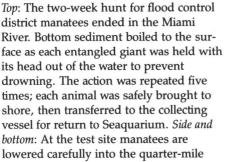

A dead manatee floated to the surface of the test section of the canal, the decomposing carcass bloated with gasses. Close inspection (*bottom*) revealed a multitude of bullet wounds and confirmed a senseless slaughter. Photos courtesy of Electa Pace, Marine Films–Medifilms.

on the supporting matrix of the water hyacinth bed, and the popping of the plants' air floats could be distinctly heard. Mechanical and chemical means of weed control suppress the effects of aquatic weeds for only one to three months. Underwater weeds removed by the manatees did not again become a serious problem until six to eight months after the manatees' feeding. The project progressed for eight months undisturbed, and the manatees even appeared to be immune to the effects of three hurricanes that passed through the area. However, the small shack that housed data recording equipment, as well as posted signs in the area, soon were riddled with bullet holes; signs and markers were torn down and thrown into the test section of the canal. The vandalism finally resulted in the project's first manatee loss. The animal was shot, then stabbed repeatedly until it was dead. Because the deceased specimen was the group's sole male, critical breeding observations were terminated. During the chill winters of 1965 and 1966, females were lost, mostly to respiratory infections. Nonetheless, the two-year project added substantially to the limited literature on West Indian manatees and the flood control district continues to educate the public about the endangered status of these harmless creatures and their unique potential as economical, efficient control agents of obnoxious aquatic weeds.

Top: Men of Tortugero, Costa Rica, butcher a female Antillean manatee, whose meat and by-products will be shared. *Bottom*: Even the baby will provide protein to a hungry people. Toenails and lack of a pink belly patch identify it as an Antillian manatee. The Tortugero area is a national park, and such hunting is against the law today. Photos courtesy of Larry Olgren, National Marine Fisheries Service, Panama City, Florida.

A more recent attempt at biological aquatic weed control took place in the beautiful canal systems in Xochimilco, the Venice of Mexico, on the southern fringes of Mexico City. The plants were blocking the passage of the *chinampas*, gaily decorated tourist barges poled by *chinamperos* through the canals to the lively tunes of mariachi musicians. The picturesque area has been a well-known gardening center since the time of the Aztecs, but its abundance of water lilies threatens to clog more than 150 miles of the area's channels. Four manatees captured in Tuxtla Gutierrez to the south and transported to Xochimilco escaped from their pen and at last report were observed a number of times consuming the lilies according to plan. A canoe patrol checks on their activities, and handbills are distributed to visitors urging them not to molest the animals if they are seen. Here again, the best protection for the manatee is a sound public education program.

Records from Brazil's Instituto Nacional de Pesquisas da Amazonia at Manaus show that at the beginning of the century some 8,000 manatees were killed over a two-year period for their highly prized meat and by-products. It has been hypothesized that over the years, without enough

WARNING TO DIVERS

The *Manatee* is an endangered species. It is fully protected by state and federal laws. Divers and swimmers may observe and enjoy these docile animals only in a manner which does not result in their disturbance.

DIVERS MAY—
—Dive in manatee areas and passively observe the animals unless the areas are specifically closed to diving.
—Come in contact (touch) manatees which approach divers for such contact.

DIVERS MAY NOT—
—Actively pursue manatees for any purpose, whether underwater or by boat.
—Attempt to ride, harness or in any way disturb, harm or harass manatees.

Divers should be aware that manatees are in these warm water areas to obtain refuge from cold water. This is necessary for the manatees to maintain their health and survive periods of very cold weather. Prolonged exposure to water under 65°F may be harmful to manatees. Any diving or boating activity which excludes manatees from these warm water refuges during critical periods may have to be curtailed. Your cooperation will help to keep these waters open for your use.

Violation of manatee protection laws may result in civil or criminal prosecution with maximum penalties of up to $20,000.00 in fines and up to one year imprisonment, or both.

Authority:
Endangered Species Act of 1973
Marine Mammal Protection Act of 1972
Florida Manatee Sanctuary Act of 1978

Florida Department of Natural Resources

manatees to control aquatic growth, weeds decaying on lake bottoms have raised hydrogen sulphide levels to a range of eutrophication intolerable to fish which are a major source of protein for people in the area. To help reverse this chain, the manatees must again prosper in this habitat. As in all countries within whose borders Sirenians are found, protective legislation has proven largely ineffective. The institute, besides undertaking research on the ecology and distribution of the Amazonian manatee, has begun a cooperative program with the organizations responsible for manatee protection to educate the public about conserving natural populations.

The National Fish and Wildlife Laboratory (NFWL) of the Fish and Wildlife Service, U.S. Department of Interior, established a field station in Gainesville, Florida, to develop an active research program in Sirenian biology. The station was staffed by full-time biologists and a number of part-time assistants who first reviewed the status of on-going Sirenian research. For U.S. populations of manatee who received first priority, a salvage program was coordinated with other interested researchers and state and federal agencies to ensure that all dead or dying manatees are located, salvaged, and analyzed. Annual surveys of the U.S. populations are being expanded to gather hard data on seasonal movements, possible migration routes, and summer population distributions. To help with such studies, ways to tag manatees both passively and sonically have been developed.

Problems of manatee-environment relationships absorb a large part of the lab's efforts in the United States. Researchers study (1) how vegetation control technology has affected manatees, (2) how manatees respond to urbanization of waterfront areas and to power plant development, and (3) what temperatures and foods are critical for manatees' winter habitat. In cooperation with the Florida Department of Natural Resources, researchers are also studying the ecological impact of manatees on restricted ecological situations to develop ways of managing manatee refuges and sanctuaries. Related studies with Florida manatees include auditory physiology and acoustic behavior, social behavior, demographic structure of manatee herds, manatee thermoregulation and metabolism, and manatees' physiological responses to diving.

In the forefront of Florida's environmental education today is the Florida Audubon Society. The society has produced a comprehensive education package of posters, bumper stickers, instructor's guide, worksheets, and videos designed to teach young people about the endangered West Indian manatee. Titled "Manatees—An Educator's Guide to the Natural History, Habitat, Problems, and Conservation of the Order Sirenia," thousands have been sent to upper elementary and middle schools, other educational institutions, and museums. The materials also have been well received by conservation groups in Guyana, Guatemala, Jamaica, Trinidad, Panama, and Belize.

WATCH OUT FOR MANATEES

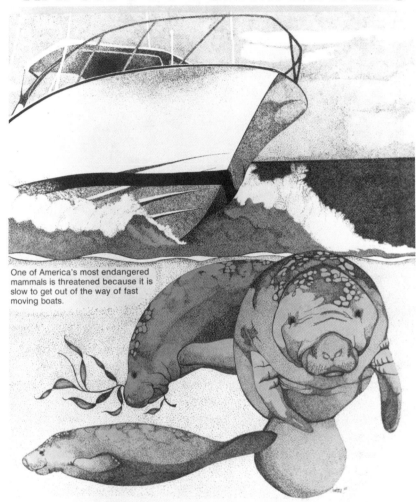

One of America's most endangered
mammals is threatened because it is
slow to get out of the way of fast
moving boats.

**HELP PROTECT THESE GENTLE AND INTERESTING ANIMALS
BY SLOWING YOUR BOAT AND BEING ON THE LOOKOUT.**

Rare Animal Relief Effort, Inc.
c/o National Audubon Society
950 Third Avenue, New York, N.Y. 10022

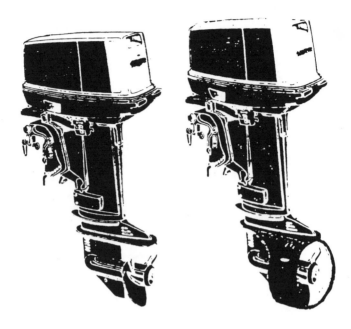

Humans remain the manatee's worst enemy, and the greatest of all human threats are the bare, whirling blades of boat propellers. (The greatest numbers of injuries from boat propellers are suffered by humans. Accidents in the many thousands among boaters, swimmers, divers, and water skiers are commonplace each year.) It would be a matter of sound business for one of the major firms to effect a redesign of the propulsion unit to reduce the incidence of human injury, and, perhaps as an inadvertent by-product, to reduce harm to aquatic creatures, among them the gentle manatees. The challenge of design stimulated these sketches of boat motors. Manufacturers report that propeller guard kits are available for outboards up to 25 horsepower; tunnelized systems with turbine-type blades are found on much larger vessels. Filling the gap between hardly seems an impossible chore.

Adjacent to Seaquarium is the University of Miami's Rosenstiel School of Marine and Atmospheric Science where staff and students study marine mammals, among them the West Indian manatee, in cooperation with the National Fish and Wildlife Laboratory in Gainesville. Under permit from the U.S. Marine Mammal Commission and the U.S. Department of the Interior, dead manatees are routinely collected and autopsied, and data are collected on pathology, pesticide, and heavy-

On January 23, 1976, to escape winter's chill, 141 manatees congregated in the warm water effluent of the Riviera Beach Power Plant, probably one of the largest such aggregations on record. This aerial photograph was taken during a population study. Photo courtesy of Nicholas Chitty.

metal samples, parasites, tissue samples, and parts or all of the skeletal structure. Researchers are trying to find a way to determine manatees' age and are studying reproductive organs to examine age at sexual maturity, longevity, mortality rates, fecundity, and growth rates. Where and how many manatees are in south Florida is being studied through aerial surveys and on-ground sighting reports. The Seaquarium herd is being studied in cooperation with the University of Florida at Gainesville in the areas of thermoregulatory physiology, endocrine physiology, electrophoresis of hemoglobin and serum proteins, female/calf behavior, and growth rates.

The cooperative efforts of the labs over several decades of study indicate that natural sea cow mortality is very low. Vandalism and other factors account for some losses, but nearly half of all mortalities were directly attributable to encounters with boats or barges. In some of my own articles I have referred to them as a mutilated species for this very reason. If these animals are to survive as a valuable aesthetic and ecological component in Florida, we must arrange some shared habitat with them. Creating sanctuaries in areas where many manatee live has proven

somewhat successful. In the early 1990s, Brevard County, one of the areas where boat collisions are common, declared itself a manatee sanctuary. The Florida Department of Natural Resources also has created a sanctuary at Blue Springs in Volusia County dedicated to peaceful coexistence between humans and manatees (see Appendix C).

Sirens through the Ages ෴

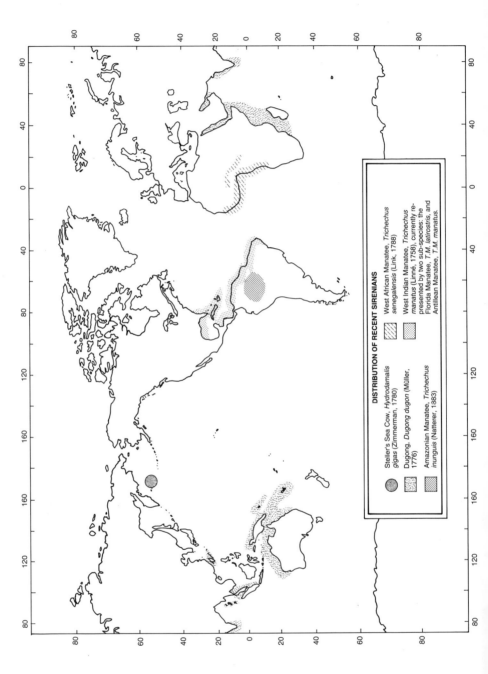

DISTRIBUTION OF RECENT SIRENIANS

Steller's Sea Cow, *Hydrodamalis gigas* (Zimmerman, 1780)

Dugong, *Dugong dugon* (Müller, 1776)

Amazonian Manatee, *Trichechus inunguis* (Natterer, 1883)

West African Manatee, *Trichechus senegalensis* (Link, 1788)

West Indian Manatee, *Trichechus manatus* (Linné, 1758), currently re-presented by two sub-species: the Florida Manatee, *T.M. latirostris*, and Antillean Manatee, *T.M. manatus*.

Aardvarks, Elephants, Hyraxes, Dugongs, and Manatees

$\mathop{\approx}\limits_{\approx}$

Sirenians are a remote order of aquatic mammals comprised of two families: Dugongidae, including the recently extinct Northern or Steller's sea cows and the surviving dugongs; and Trichechidae, the manatees. These little understood, strange, innocuous, wholly aquatic creatures are classified taxonomically within the superorder that includes aardvarks, elephants, and hyraxes.

Aardvarks defy sensible description; visualize a large, naked, nocturnal mammal that appears to be a cross between a huge-eared jackrabbit and a wrinkly Mexican hairless with the food preference of an anteater. Elephants hardly require description. Hyraxes, referred to as "conies" in the Bible, probably are as endemic to secluded terrestrial habitats as are their Sirenian cousins in the aquatic domain. They are small, hooved, furry, 8- to 10-pound mammals found living in rocky cliff areas of Africa. Dugongs and manatees, aardvarks, elephants, and hyraxes are diverse creatures that share specific physiological characteristics in spite of the incongruity of their general appearance. Fossil evidence suggests that 25 to 60 million years ago all of these orders ascended from a common stock, one branch of which remained on dry land while the other returned to the water. Of the latter, Northern sea cows were, and dugongs still are, entirely marine, and manatees are confined to fresh waters (euryhaline).

The dawn beast (Eotherium) and the dawn siren (Eosiren) were ancestral Sirenian forms from the Eocene fossil beds of Egypt. Intensive archeological exploration of these marine and estuarine deposits has uncovered a relative abundance of fossils of these two creatures. This abundance must not be misconstrued to mean that this Egyptian site is the seat of the order, for the true place of origin of any given mammalian order is uncertain. If Africa did give rise to the sirens, migration from this

Representative members of the Superorder Paenungulata are the hyraxes, manatees, dugongs, and elephants, unlikely companions that share a common branch on the tree of life. *Top*: African elephant, *Loxodonta africana*. Photo courtesy of Gordon Hubbel, D.V.M. *Center*: Rock hyrax, *Procavia capensis*. Photo courtesy of Crandon Park Zoo. *Bottom*: West Indian manatee, subspecies *Trichechus manatus latirostris*. Photo courtesy of Miami Seaquarium.

Opposite page—Top, right: Steller's sea cow, *Hydrodamalis gigas* (Zimmerman, 1780). This composite skeleton was assembled from bones salvaged on the beaches of Bering Island in 1883. *Center, right*: Dugong, *Dugong dugon* (Müller, 1776). Unknown numbers of this species range coastal waters of the Indian Ocean, the East Indies, and the western Pacific. *Bottom, right*: West Indian manatee, *Trichechus manatus* (Linne, 1758). Manatees currently are represented by two subspecies, the Florida manatee, *T. m. latirostris*, and the Antillean manatee, *T. m. manatus*. Photos courtesy of James Mead, Ph.D., curator of mammals, Smithsonian Institution, Washington, D.C.

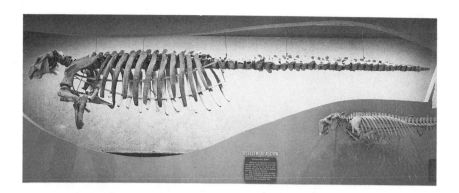

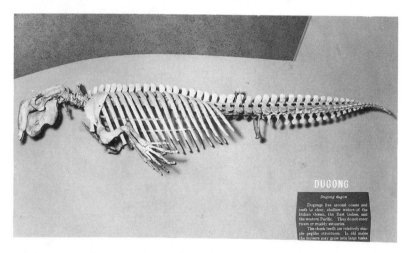

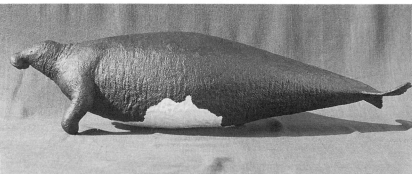

These photographs of Steller's sea cow, *Hydrodamalis gigas* (Zimmerman, 1780) are of a 1:12 scale model developed by paleontologist Daryl Domning from fossil skeletons and archive data and executed by sculptor Pamela Vesterby of Berkeley, California. Photos courtesy of Pamela Vesterby.

ancient home must have been rapid, archeologically speaking. Early forms have been found in sites ranging from Italy, France, Belgium, Austria, Germany, and England to the West Indies and California. Mostly, these were ancestors of dugongs whose broad ranges would lead one to believe they must have inhabited the warm, shallow, coastal waters

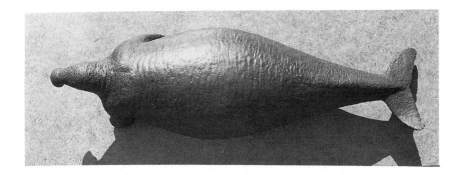

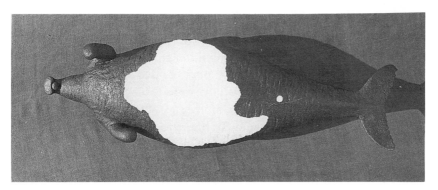

of nearly all continents. The fossil record of manatees is more difficult to trace, but it has been determined that late in the Tertiary (to one million years ago) they and the dugongs coexisted in Florida. Both modern dugongs and manatees are found in Africa, but manatees alone survive on Atlantic coasts.

Sirens, both dugongs and manatees, seem well adapted to life in shallow water; their shape and structure have become suited to this form of environment through evolutionary development. Their bodies have lost the hind limbs but do retain internal pelvic vestiges, proof that these mammals once were terrestrial creatures that migrated millions of years ago to the aquatic environment. Having lost the need for hind limbs, the animals lost all traces of them but the vestiges of the pelvis. Except for their paddle shape, in form and position the creatures' forelimbs are rather like those of land mammals and are highly mobile with the exception of the wrist joint. These flexible forelimbs permit a kind of walking motion on the bottom. In all but dugongs and freshwater Amazon manatees, siren forelimbs are tipped with thick, heavy nails. The blimp-shaped body terminates in a whalelike, crescent-shaped tail in dugongs or a broad, rounded paddle in manatees. The tail and the specialized forelimbs provide most of a siren's locomotion. Swimming is accomplished by an undulating body motion accompanied by powerful vertical thrusts of the tail. Paddling motions of the forelimbs accomplish turns, and sculling with one or the other limb will guide the beast right or left. A twist of the tail in either direction yields the same result. An almost imperceptible body arch or tilt of the tail directs the creature up or down. At rest, a siren seems no more than a clumsy beast, but size and ungainly shape belie a delightful grace of motion as fluid as the water in which it moves.

Peculiar to this order of mammal are the pectoral mammaries. A single breast is located at the posterior margin of the juncture of each forelimb and the body. To nurse, the Sirenian baby grasps this location with its strong lips. Its body position parallels that of the mother, or cow, maintaining a relatively undisturbed hydrodynamic configuration. Firmly affixed, lips to breast, offspring and mother are able to rest on the bottom, float on or near the surface, or swim harmoniously in unison. Were the pectoral mammaries in the pelvic region, as in horses and cattle, progress in any direction would be impossible against the back pressure of the water.

Peculiar to sea cows (the vernacular for all dugongs and manatees today) is the partial or even total loss of spongiosa (less dense bone) and marrow cavity, yielding bone of greater density. The resultant weight increase offsets positive bouyancy; voluntary changes in lung air volume allow the animal to adjust its depth in the water column without body movement. This characteristic, coupled with a lengthened vertebral column and shifts in the topography of internal organs, yields a structure that is well adapted to the animal's environmental requirements.

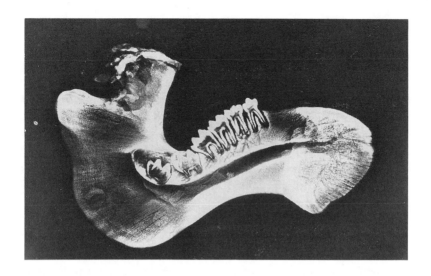

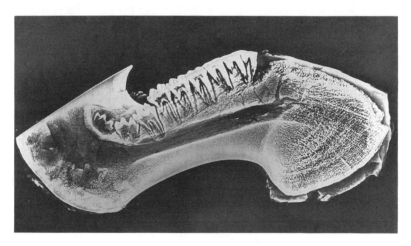

Top: Xeroradiograph of the lower jaw of a manatee 5 feet 11 inches long in which no teeth have been replaced, as indicated by lack of wear on the front molar. Note the two unerupted molars forming toward the rear of the jaw. *Bottom*: The jaw of an older manatee 10 feet 5 inches long in which tooth replacement has started. Note the crown wear and root resorption progressing toward the front. Xeroradiography by Louis Selzer, U.S.C. Dental School; photo by Daniel Odell, Ph.D. Courtesy of The Johns Hopkins University Press.

Sirenian facial features are unique. Beady, small, sphincterlike myopic-appearing eyes give sirens a countenance that brings to mind some lovable cartoon character. Ears are lacking, and only Dugongidae have external ear holes visible. In manatees, these are closed but may show as minute pits. Sirens do hear well, communicating audibly to the human ear with high-pitched chirps that would sound far more appropriate emanating from sparrows than from 1,200-pound mammals. Nostrils are valvelike and remain tightly closed while the animal is submerged. No less curious are the bristly lips; the upper lip is cleft, and each half is capable of moving independently of the other. They are highly efficient food-gathering mechanisms.

Several striking differences exist between dugongs' and manatees' teeth. Dugongs bear a pair of long upper tusks and three functional cheek teeth, or molars, in each mouth quadrant in younger animals; with age, the forward molar is lost, leaving only two in each quadrant. Wear does not mean that the animals lose teeth and grow new ones. Instead, as the top or crown of a tooth is worn, it continually grows above the gum line to remain functional. Manatees, on the other hand, have rudimentary incisors concealed beneath the horny plate that are lost before maturity. They have more molars, seven or eight per quadrant at any given time, and a curious way of replacing teeth. New teeth form and erupt at the rear of the tooth row as worn teeth are shed at the front, the entire row moving forward: bone between the teeth is absorbed, and the teeth migrate to their new position, with bone being redeposited between them to re-anchor them there. This combination of horizontal movement with an apparently limitless supply of molars is unique to manatees; it is found in no other mammal, not even other Sirenians.

Steller's Sea Cows and Dugongs ⌇⌇

Steller's Sea Cow

Steller's sea cows (*Hydrodamalis gigas* [Zimmerman, 1780]) were immense creatures discovered off Copper and Bering islands in the Bering Sea in 1741 by the explorer Captain Vitus Bering. The main purpose of his voyage was to chart a passage across the North Pacific to America. The ship's log of his ill-fated vessel, *St. Peter,* and a manuscript in the archives of the Russian Academy of Sciences at St. Petersburg document the difficult journey. As the end of the voyage neared, the *St. Peter* was wrecked. The commander lost his life; both the Bering Sea and Bering Island upon which the survivors were cast still bear his name. The giant sea cows they discovered were named for the German naturalist who had sailed with Bering, George Wilhelm Steller, the only trained naturalist ever to study these creatures in their natural environment. The sea cow Steller describes in his *De bestiis marinis* reminds one of the odd African wildebeest, an animal reputed to have been "assembled by a committee."

Steller wrote that the front of the sea cow resembled a seal, the rear half was fishlike, the head like that of a buffalo, the skull like that of a horse, and that it had no teeth except for two strong horny plates used to grind up seaweed. It had lips covered with thick bristles. It had tiny eyes and small auditory orifices. Its neck was short and thick. The nailless front paws with their two joints lacked phalanges and looked as if they had been amputated at the ends and doubled under into hooks. With these clublike paws the animal pulled itself along the bottom in shallow water; they were not used for swimming. In fact, the animal moved on the surface, back awash, and never was observed to dive. The stubby forelimbs also served as clubs with which the animal knocked loose the holdfasts of kelp and other algae that comprised its diet. Steller said the sea cow's back was like that of an ox, its flanks and belly rounded, and that its tail grew thinner toward the flukes, which were flat, horizontal, and forked like those of a whale.

Steller's notes on the habits of sea cows make them seem quite real. They always lived in shallow areas of the sea, he wrote, chiefly in locales where freshwater streams emptied into the ocean.

These animals, like cattle, live in herds at sea, males and females going together and driving the young before them along shore. They are occupied with nothing else but their food. They eat in the same manner as the land animals, with a slow forward movement. They tear the seaweed from the rocks and chew it without cessation. However, the structure of the stomach taught me that they do not ruminate, as I had first supposed. During the eating they move the head and neck like an ox, and after the lapse of a few minutes they lift the head out of the water and draw fresh air with a rasping and snorting sound after the manner of horses. When the tide falls, they go away from the land to sea, but with the rising tide go back again to the shore, often so near that we could strike and reach them with poles from shore. They are not afraid of man in the least, nor do they seem to hear very poorly. Signs of a wonderful intelligence I could not observe, but indeed an uncommon love for one another, which even extended so far that when one of them was hooked, all the other were intent upon saving him. They tried to prevent the wounded companion from being drawn on the beach by forming a closed circle around him; some attempted to upset the yawl; others laid themselves over the rope or tried to pull the harpoon out of his body, in which intent they succeeded several times. We also noticed, not without astonishment, that a male came two days to a female which was lying dead on the beach, as if he would inform himself about her condition. Nevertheless, no matter how many of them were wounded or killed, they always remained in one place.

Their mating takes place in June, with protracted preludes. The female moves slowly before the male with continual turns about, but the male pursues her without cessation. When these animals move to take a rest on the water, they lie on their backs in a quiet place and allow themselves to drift on to the sea like logs.

These animals are found at all seasons of the year everywhere around the island in great numbers, so that the whole population of the eastern coast of Kamchatka [will] always be able to keep itself more than abundantly supplied from them with fat and meat.

Steller wrote that the skin is uncommonly thick,

more like the bark of an oak than the skin of an animal, black, rough, wrinkled, like stone, hard, tough, and hairless which one can hardly do anything to even with an axe or hook and if one cuts it across, it is completely like ebony in smoothness and color. This outer rind is not, however, the skin but a cuticle and smooth on the back. This thick outer skin seems to have been given to it originally chiefly for two reasons. (1) So that, because it lives in rocky and rough places, and in the winter among the ice, it should be able to feed without the skin being knocked off; or they are fitted with this armor so that when they are cast against rocks by large waves, as I have often seen, they should not be killed. (2) So that their body heat should not escape so rapidly in summer through strong evaporation, or in the winter be wholly suppressed by the cold. For unlike other animals and fish, they are not able to remain in the depths of the sea, but when searching for food must always expose half their bodies to the cold.

This cuticle is constantly attacked and infested by insects on the head, the eyes, the ears, the breasts and under the arms where it is rough, which also frequently pierce through the cuticle and damage the skin itself. These attract sea gulls which sit on the animal's backs and seek with their sharp beaks after this, to them agreeable food, and thus render a friendly and pleasant service to the tormented animals.

The "insects" later were determined to be small parasitic crustaceans (amphepodes, *Cyamus rhytinae*).

Sea cows' ancestors had reached their widest Pacific geographic distribution by the middle of the late Pliocene (5 million years), ranging from the Islands of Japan around North Pacific coasts to northern Mexico. Fossil records indicate that as recently as 20,000 years ago their range extended southward as far as Monterey in central California.

Within that comparatively brief time frame until the mid-eighteenth century, sea cows were reduced to the small relict Bering Sea population found by Steller. Logic suggests that the sole survival factor that favored the population in so foreboding an area as the terminus of the Aleutian arc is that the locale remained unknown to and uninhabited by ancient or modern humans until the eighteenth century. Once discovered and reported living in waters surrounding islands rich in furbearing animals, such as foxes and sea otters, their demise was assured. For hunters followed and they, as did the marooned men of the Bering expedition, found sea cow meat nourishing and almost indistinguishable from beef in taste. Fat rendered an oil much like that of sweet almonds. Adult sea cows grew to up to 30 feet and possibly 10 tons, enough to provide sustenance for dozens of men for weeks at a time. A large hunting party could harpoon or hook an adult cow and with effort haul it ashore for butchering. More often than not, a wasteful alternative was employed. The beast was impaled and left to die, hopefully to drift ashore on an incoming tide. If it sank or was carried elsewhere by currents, the hunter or hunting party simply impaled another and again hoped for the best. With what would have seemed an abundance of easy prey, and faced with a task akin to butchering an elephant while standing in icy water, one suspects that often no more than choice portions of the carcass were harvested. The entire population at the time, however, probably was no more than 1,500 to 2,000 animals, so hunters were forced to turn their efforts to less docile game. Not that Steller's sea cows were wiped off the earth in a quarter of a century. These hunts simply brought down the final curtain on a lengthy attrition that lasted many thousands of years. Presumably, the extermination pattern would have followed that of the expansion of human culture: the Japanese archipelago northward, then the coasts of Mexico and California, and north to the end of the Aleutian chain.

The total evidence for this story consists of Steller's notes, a rather limited number of scientific papers, and in the museums of the world, about a dozen fossil skeletons, each of which has been reconstructed from parts of more than one animal. I include the story to reinforce a simple, basic message: Steller's sea cows possibly numbered 2,000 when discovered by Bering and Steller; soon they were gone. Today there are thought to be no more than 1,800 manatees left in Florida. Without public awareness of their endangered status, how long will it take human beings to eradicate them from the path of continually expanding civilization?

Dugongs

So strange a beast was the dugong that it stirred the fertile mind of Jules Verne in his 1875 classic adventure tale, "The Mysterious Island."

The colonists were about to begin to traverse the plateau to return to the Chimneys, when Top gave new signs of agitation. He barked with fury, and before his master could restrain him, he had plunged a second time into the lake.

All ran toward the bank. The dog was already more than twenty feet off and Cyrus was calling him back when an enormous head emerged from the water, which did not appear to be deep in that place.

Herbert recognized directly the species of amphibian to which the tapering head, with large eyes and adorned with long silky mustaches, belonged.

—A lamantin! he cried.

It was not a lamantin, but one of that species of the order of cetaceans, which bear the name of the "dugong," for its nostrils were open at the upper part of its snout. The enormous animal rushed on the dog, who tried to escape by returning toward the shore. His master could do nothing to save him, and before Gideon Spilett or Herbert thought of bending their bows, Top, seized by the dugong, had disappeared beneath the water.

Neb, his iron-tipped spear in his hand, wished to go to Top's help, and attack the dangerous animal in its own element.

—No Neb,—said the engineer, restraining his courageous servant.

Meanwhile, a struggle was going on beneath the water, an explicable struggle, for in his situation Top could not possibly resist; and judging by the bubbling of the surface, it must be also a terrible struggle, and could not but terminate in the death of the dog!

But suddenly, in the middle of a foaming circle, Top appeared. Thrown in the air by some unknown power, he rose ten feet above the surface of the lake, fell again into the midst of the agitated waters, and then soon gained the shore without any severe wounds, miraculously saved.

Cyrus Harding and his companions could not understand it. What was not less inexplicable was that the struggle still appeared to be going on. Doubtless, the dugong, attacked by some powerful animal, after having released the dog, was fighting on his own account. But it did not last long. The water became red with blood, and the body of the dugong, emerging from the sheet of scarlet which spread around, soon stranded on a little beach at the south angle of the lake. The colonists ran toward it. The dugong was dead. It was an enormous animal, fifteen or sixteen feet long, and must have weighed from three to four thousand pounds. At its neck was a wound, which appeared to have been produced by a sharp blade.

What could the amphibious creature have been, who by this terrible blow had destroyed the formidable dugong? No one could tell, and much interested in this incident, Harding and his companions returned to the Chimneys.

The next day, the 7th of May, Harding and Gideon Spilett, leaving Neb to prepare breakfast, climbed Prospect Heights, while Herbert and Pencroft ascended by the river, to renew their store of wood.

The engineer and the reporter soon reached the little beach on which the dugong had been stranded. Already flocks of birds had attacked the mass of flesh, and had to be driven away with stones, for Cyrus wished to keep the fat for the use of the colony. As to the animal's flesh, it would furnish excellent food, for in the islands of the Malay archipelago and elsewhere, it is especially reserved for the table of the native princess.

The taxonomy of dugongs has been subject to scrutiny for some two hundred years, beginning with a reference in the literature to the Indian dugong, *Dugong dugon* (Müller, 1776). Thereafter, these marine sirenians were classified and reclassified and were grouped in the case of vernacular names according to their widespread geographic distribution. There was the Australian dugong, *Dugong australis*, the East African dugong, *Halicore dugong* (Illiger, 1811), and the Indian dugong, *Halicore australe* (Owen, 1847). That looks more confusing than it is; generic nomenclature was changed from *Dugong* to *Halicore* and species were considered diverse enough in taxonomic variations to be separated and in geographic range not to comprise interbreeding groups, two basic criteria for defining species. However, data compiled worldwide for two centuries have led workers in the field to agree that the variations recorded are not significant enough for individual species classification. Today all such animals are referred to simply as dugongs, from the Malay name *doyong*. (The meaning of the word *doyong* is lost among the myriad dialects of the native tongue.)

Dugongs do not grow to immense proportions as did the Steller's sea cows. Adults might reach 9½ feet and 800 pounds. Their general body shape is fusiform, tapering toward each end. The head is blunt and massive, with little more than a neck skin furrow and bulbous chin ventrally to demarcate the head from the rest of the body. The back of the body tapers to notched flukes midway along the sides. Overall, dugong configuration is rather like that of a whale, except for the unique blunt bulbous muzzle that comprises the bulk of the head. The upper lips form a large horseshoe-shaped bristly disc. A knob of compact fibrous connective tissue protrudes between the disc and the top of the mouth. Long coarse bristles project toward the back of the jaws on either side of this knob and interlock with those on the fleshy lower lip.

Within the mouth are two pairs of deeply rooted incisor teeth. The inner pair is absorbed, the outer pair penetrate the gums slightly as strong tusks. There are five or six molars in each jaw, but only two or three of these cheek teeth are functional at a time. Their roots are simple and open,

An immature female dugong (6 feet, 3 inches), accidentally caught and drowned in a shark net set at Picnic Bay, Magnetic Island, Queensland, in May 1975. Her death provided opportunity for scientific research. Photo courtesy of George Heinsohn, Ph.D., James Cook University of North Queensland.

Both halves of the dugong's upper snout are capable of independent movement that directs food into the mouth. The facial disc is thought to be used in uprooting tubers and roots, as evidenced by tusk wear on males and on those females with erupted tusks. Photo courtesy of George Heinsohn, Ph.D., James Cook University of North Queensland, Townsville, Queensland, Australia.

and the teeth lack enamel, being composed of cementum and orthodentine. Beneath the horny tissue in the apparently toothless anterior arc of the jaw are six vestigial incisors and two vestigial canines. None of these ever break through the gum. The entire front and mouth area of the face is directed ventrally, an adaptation for bottom feeding. Small crescent-shaped nostrils open at the upper surface of the snout. These cannot close completely, but nasal duct muscles contract or relax to close the passages to keep water out or to open them for breathing.

Tissue in the lungs of dugongs contains unique vesicles, small cells or

Lateral view of a dugong head displays the sphincterlike eye, bristles, and protruding disc of compact fibrous connective tissue. The ventrally directed mouth has evolved for bottom feeding. Photo courtesy of Steinhart Aquarium, California Academy of Sciences, San Francisco, California.

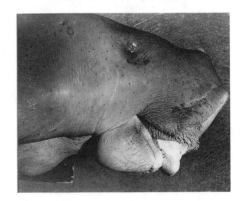

This immature female dugong, 6 feet, 9 inches, drowned in a fishing net set off Magnetic Island near Townsville, Australia, in June 1974. Note the lack of nails on the forelimbs and the pectoral mammaries at the rear margin of the base of the limb. Photo courtesy of George Heinsohn, Ph.D., James Cook University of North Queensland, Townsville, Queensland, Australia.

cavities that arise laterally along the thin-walled, tubular extensions of the windpipe, rather than the grape-clusterlike air cells, or alveoli, common to most mammals' lungs. The large, globular heart is considered primitive. Its blood's usually low oxygen-combining capacity may be responsible for the dugong's sluggish way of life.

As with Sirenians in general, hind limbs are absent, the pelvic girdle is vestigial, and nailless forelimbs are paddlelike. The dugong has neither eyelashes nor discernible upper and lower lids. Its eyes open and close with a sphincter motion rather like a shutter on a camera lens. Nictitating membranes slide closed over the eyes from front to rear. Glands provide a copious flow of viscous tears, particularly apparent when the animal is removed from the water.

The umbilicus is located in the center of the abdomen. Testes are abdominal and the sheathed penis is near the umbilicus. The genital opening of the female is located farther back, close to the anus.

The dugong's skin is extremely thick and quite smooth compared to the manatee's. In the very young it is pale cream in color, darkening with age to a slate color on the back and a paler gray on the stomach. The skin invariably is scarred, cut, and scratched from inadvertent encounters with corals, shells, and other sharp objects. Although the shark is assumed to be a dugong's sole natural predator, dugongs seldom display the shark bite's curved, ugly scars found so often on other marine mammals.

Dugongs are saltwater mammals. Although they have been found in brackish coastal waters and are able to survive in fresh water, they are not known to swim up rivers. Generally, they confine their range to coastal waters of from two to three fathoms, or twelve to eighteen feet. Here, nutrient-rich silts and sand support healthy plant growth where the vegetarian dugong can graze. Here, too, bays, lagoons, and outer protective coral reefs provide sheltered seas. Being secretive and timid creatures, the dugongs spend their days hidden in deeper water offshore. With the onset of darkness, they move into the shallow pastures through safe swimways to spend the night feeding until dawn's first light.

Dugongs' usual short diurnal movements become larger inshore migrations in areas where monsoons or similar violent storms are likely to occur. Seasonal migrations covering greater distances are not normal, but if normal pastures are destroyed by storms, the animals must move to other feeding areas or starve. The only other circumstance that we know has caused lengthy migrations and shrinking herds has been the expansion of civilization. In contrast to the limited numbers of Steller's sea cows, earlier victims of human ignorance, the most widespread and least rare of modern Sirenians are the dugongs of the Indo-Pacific region. They have, however, suffered so seriously in recent times from human depredations that now, over much of their range, they must be considered rare.

Along the east coast of Africa, dugongs may be found here and there from Egypt, in the Red Sea, south to areas of Mozambique and are most abundant in Kenya and the Somali Republic. They have also been reported from the Persian Gulf and along the west coast of India. In the Gulf of Mannar, between India and Sri Lanka, they were once abundant enough to support a commercial fishery. They still occur in Sri Lanka and range through the Andaman Islands, the Mergui Archipelago, Burma, Malaysia, the Maluas, and Sumatra. A few can be found in the Ryukyu Archipelago, and their present range extends south and east to include Guam, the Palau Islands, the Carolines, New Britain, New Guinea, the Solomons, New Caledonia, and New Hebrides. In Australia, dugongs

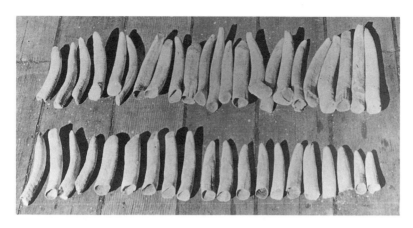

These dugongs tusks from Thursday Island in the Torres Straits between New Guinea and Australia are highly prized by the islanders, as are all parts of the useful marine mammal. Photo courtesy of G. C. L. Bertram, Ph.D.

occur from Brisbane in the east around the northern coast to Perth on the west. The populations off the northern Australian coast in Shark Bay, Broome, the Gulf of Carpentaria, and along the coast of Queensland appear to be maintaining themselves and may even be increasing.

Dugongs are subject to human exploitation for many reasons. Their flesh is sought as a source of protein and is reputed to have the flavor of veal or pork and the great advantage of being rather resistant to spoilage. Rolled and smoked it is said to taste like bacon. In certain Asiatic Pacific islands, dugongs were taken as tribute to feudal lords, and Jules Verne wrote that their meat was "reserved for the table of the native princess." Fishermen of Sri Lanka believed the meat was an aphrodisiac that would make one young again. The meat was especially desired by Moslems, who used it as a pork substitute. Ceylonese demand in the mid-1800s caused prices to soar; live animals were shipped to the markets by rail. During World War II, dugong in the western Pacific north of Australia, especially in the Palau Islands, were almost exterminated.

In biblical days, the Ark of the Covenant was said to have been protected during its travels in the Sinai by a shield of tough dugong skin. Ancient inscriptions describe palaces of kings having been built as elaborate tentlike structures with coverings of sea cowhides. The thick durable leather has long been used for soles of sandals by people on the Red Sea coast, as well.

Up to eight gallons of oil can be rendered from the average adult animal. Similar to cod liver oil, it serves a multitude of purposes and, particularly to the minds of Australian aborigines, possesses valuable medicinal qualities, having extraordinary powers of penetration. Dugong fat, administered in the form of a sweetmeat, is said by fishermen of Sri Lanka to help cure dysentery. The Mohorrais of Madagascar use dugong body fat for skin diseases, including leprosy, and mixed with rice as a laxative. They use fat taken from the head as a calmative for headaches and earaches. Powder ground from the last rib, the Mohorrais have found, combats lung ailments, and that from the tusks cleanses those who have transgressed a food taboo. The Chinese prized the tympanic bones of dugongs' middle ears as medicine. Finely powdered, they were taken to clear the kidneys of obstructions and afflictions. Comoro Islanders use powdered bones to cure ulcers. In Malaysia, the copious tears secreted by these sirens were collected and highly prized as an aphrodisiac.

As dugong populations shrank, the dugong fisheries shut down in the late nineteenth and early twentieth centuries. Demand still exists in certain limited markets, but now the animals legally may be taken only by native peoples for whom harpooning the dugong is a traditional way of life, among them islanders of the Torres Straits and aborigines on the Australian coast.

Dugongs still die by means other than natural calamities such as monsoons. Offshore boat traffic takes its toll, increased fisheries activities have resulted in accidental drownings, dynamite fishing inadvertently causes deaths, and shark-netting programs off African and Australian coasts result in numerous drownings. Protective regulations, although difficult to enforce, are in effect in Egypt, Anglo-Egyptian Sudan, Ethiopia, Somalia, Kenya, Tanzania, Mozambique, Madagascar, South Africa, Natal, India, Sri Lanka, Sabah, Sarawak, the Philippines, Japan, Formosa, New Caledonia, and Australia.

Probably the first and only dugong ever brought alive to an aquarium in the United States was Eugenie, the dugong mermaid, who in 1955 captured the interest and hearts of millions of television and newsreel viewers and visitors to Steinhart Aquarium in San Francisco. Unlike some dugongs who have thrived for more than a dozen years in a captive environment, Eugenie, from the very start of her story, was destined to be shortlived.

Eugenie's tale began in the Palau Islands north of New Guinea and east of the Philippines with the expedition Project Coral Fish, sponsored

A stylized carving of a dugong from the Trobriand Islands, New Guinea. The piece is in the collection of Brydget E. T. Hudson, ecologist, Education, Konedoru, New Guinea. Photo by Office of Information, Papua New Guinea.

by the George Vanderbilt Foundation, the Office of Naval Research, Trust and Territory Government of the Pacific Islands, and the Pacific Science Board (National Research Council–National Academy of Sciences).

In vain, expedition members searched all likely areas for a glimpse of their elusive quarry. Only one week before their scheduled departure, a Palauan brought in a 5½-foot, 180-pound dugong. The animal had been speared between the tail and the vital organs, then hauled aboard a canoe for the two-hour return trip to the island under the hot tropical sun. Upon arrival, the proud native hunters decided to show off their prize and drove it in a jeep over bumpy island roads to place it in an abandoned Japanese swimming pool filled with seawater that fluctuated with the tide.

A Torres Strait islander displays his *wap*, a dugong harpoon hurled from either a canoe or a platform constructed on the reef. The hunter walks the reef in daytime searching for a patch of partially browsed dugong grass. Knowing that the dugong will return until the fodder is exhausted, he erects the staging and waits through the night for his prey. A wooden or stone image on the platform serves as a charm to ensure its return. Because the harpoon head seldom penetrates to vital organs, the hunter or his companions must tie a second rope around the dugong's tail and hold the animal underwater until it drowns. Photo by G.C.L. Bertram, Ph.D.

Expedition members learned of the prize and immediately went to the pool, where the dugong swam slowly around showing no signs of distress after its ordeal. A number of islanders, mostly children, began upsetting the animal by swimming with it, but by the next day it no longer reacted to the antics of its playmates. The expedition bought the dugong from the Palauans and, assured by the natives that it was a female, named it Eugenie in honor of Eugenie Clark, who had written about a dugong in the Red Sea in "Lady with a Spear." Food had to be provided—eel grass, clams, and white sea cucumbers. The cucumbers are considered a delicacy by the natives, and a number of children were caught competing with Eugenie for them on the bottom of the pool. (If clams and sea cucumbers were considered by expedition scientists to be dietary staples for the dugong, should the animals be considered meateaters as well as vegetarians? Most of the research literature says no, and votes them vegetarians.)

"The dugong industry is being rapidly developed in the State of Queensland [in 1924] and is proving a most important asset. In the North West the blacks hunt these sea cows on a rough raft constructed of mangrove saplings pinned together with hard wood pegs." Photo from *National Geographic*, March 1924, © National Geographic Society.

The plan was to ship Eugenie to Earl S. Herald, curator of the Steinhart Aquarium and a trustee of the George Vanderbilt Foundation. There, the dugong would provide an educational public exhibit, and its habits could be studied further under controlled conditions. Meanwhile, Eugenie became something of a celebrity in her home territory. Most Palauans had never seen such an oddity. Their knowledge of dugongs had been passed down by elders who had seen large herds inhabiting their waters. Young and old flocked day after day from all corners of the islands to marvel.

Finally, snug in her foam-padded box, Eugenie was flown to Guam. She spent the half-day layover while awaiting the flight to San Francisco splashing about in a large water-filled life raft in the air terminal lobby. In San Francisco, Earl Herald met her with an aquarium truck outfitted with another life raft filled with 85° F sea water, exactly the temperature of her lagoon water in the Palaus. Eugenie was whisked away to her new home amid the whir of newsreel and television cameras, the darling of the West Coast.

On the morning of December 27, 1955, within months of her capture, Eugenie died as a consequence of her original spear wounds. Autopsy

"This specimen was 12 feet in length and weighed about 600 pounds. Over 50 years ago it was said that the mammals could be speared at almost any point on the Australian coast and the flesh was eaten by whites and blacks alike." Photo from *National Geographic*, March 1924, © National Geographic Society.

These dugongs were taken by aborigines at Dugong Bay, Australia. They are "caught like the whale but, owing to the great thickness of its hide, many spears were turned and broken, so the hunting is not always carried out with success." Photo from *National Geographic*, March 1924, © National Geographic Society.

Three dugongs, dead and bloated on shore, drowned entangled in a shark net at Picnic Bay, Magnetic Island, Queensland, February 29, 1972. *Back, left to right*: an adult female (8 feet 4 inches) and an adult male (8 feet 4½ inches). *Foreground*: subadult male (6 feet 7 inches). Photo courtesy of George Heinsohn, Ph.D., James Cook University of North Queensland, Queensland, Australia.

A dugong conservation poster's message in English is reinforced in native dialect on the Papuan badge. This educational material is distributed throughout New Guinea courtesy of Rare Animal Relief Effort, Inc., New York.

THE DUGONG

one of Papua New Guinea's NATIONAL ANIMALS

PROTECT DUGONGS
IN YOUR PROVINCE

Papuan postage stamps reinforce the conservation message and heighten world awareness of the dugong's existence. Photo by the author.

revealed gangrene in the area of spear damage to the spinal column. Still, the heroic efforts of expedition members and of Earl Herald and his staff were not in vain. Scientists added substantially to data on *Dugong dugon*, and the public had been introduced to one of the world's most interesting yet least known animals.

Some thirty-five years later, during the summer of 1980 while I was director of Seaquarium in Miami, several gentlemen from the Toba Aquarium in Toba, Japan, visited Seaquarium during my absence. They left behind their guide book, which I perused with interest upon my return, especially as it included an artist's rendition of a dugong. Unable to read the text, I wrote to Teruo Kataoka, Toba's assistant director, who had left the book. I asked whether he had photographs of a live specimen, and to my absolute delight, data and photographs of Toba's two live and healthy specimens soon were in my hands.

Both Toba dugongs had been taken in the Luzon Islands, Philippines, the female in May 1977 and the male in September 1979. Each has thrived on a diet of 22 to 28.6 pounds per day of sea grass, *Zostera marina*. Their marine aquarium measures 36 by 18 by 7.2 feet and holds about 35,500 gallons of water. Salinity is 20.20 to 34.72 percent at 80.6° to 84.2° F.

A male and a female dugong from the seas off Luzon, Phillipines, loll in their 35,000-gallon aquarium in Toba, Japan. The 36-foot-wide thick plexiglass viewing window is free of mullions and provides unimpeded viewing for visitors and scientific observers. Photos courtesy of Toba Aquarium.

	Date	Length (inches)	Weight (pounds)
Female	May 20, 1977	65.35	164.34
	January 20, 1979	71.26	217.14
	November 10, 1979	74.80	242.00
	April 21, 1980	75.20	316.80
Male	September 11, 1979	66.93	178.20
	March 25, 1980	67.48	180.40

Dugongs still are on display in Toba, Japan, as well as in Surabaya and Jakarta, Indonesia. While captive breeding programs have not yet proved successful, there is little doubt that viable offspring soon will become a reality, and many questions regarding the husbandry of these fascinating mammals will be answered.

Amazonian and West
African Manatees ≋≋

Amazonian Manatee

At the Zoological Gardens of Philadelphia in 1873, two Amazonian manatees (*Trichechus inunguis* [Natterer, 1883]) lived for two and one-half months in the earliest attempt at maintaining captured specimens. In a third attempt during the summer of 1876, the manatee survived for just under three months. A young male and female manatee were on exhibit at the Brighton Aquarium in England at about this same time. These two animals had been taken in South America and were referred to as *Manatus americanus,* and descriptive literature concerning them indicates that the pair were Amazonian manatees.

In the twentieth century, three Amazonian manatees were held at the New York Aquarium in 1939 and 1940. The first, a baby, was described by director Christopher Coates in the *Bulletin of the New York Zoological Society.* I include his notes with few omissions because, as he stated, nothing was known at the time "of the living of these animals and it is only by the reporting of the minutiae of such behavior as may be observed that we will ever know anything of them."

> The classical mermaid is more beautiful than Badoura [in the *Arabian Nights,* the "most beautiful woman on earth"]; a sort of combination of Aphrodite and Andromeda—the epitome of maidenly loveliness and gentleness—the unknowable and unidentifiable desire of all mankind, down to her waist. Below her waist she has glitter, grace and power in her silvery-green fish tail.
>
> The traditional position of such a creature is to be seated upon a wave-washed rock in the midst of a calm, intensely blue, tropic sea, and the traditional occupation is to comb her long golden hair the while she sings of the ineffable delights and felicities of the universe in a voice which might well be the envy of Euterpe.

If approached too closely by boisterous mankind, she modestly slid off her rock and as effortlessly as an eagle soaring, sought refuge in her father's palace at the bottom of the water, an abode which seems to have been uncomfortably cluttered with strings of pearls and red coral arm-chairs.

While such a concept can only exist in the minds of men who desire they know not what, one would be surprised at the number of people who ask Aquarium attendants, in all seriousness, where we keep the mermaid and who are genuinely disappointed and sometimes indignant, when informed that these are mythical creatures. . . .

The Aquarium had a mermaid—that is, it had a manatee. This manatee was of the species which had not been included in the group of mermaid-myth animals because its native area, and all the inhabitants thereof, were not only undiscovered, but were undreamed-of when the mermaid myths were in the making. If the following notes on this creature seem unnecessarily detailed, we ask indulgence and return to our statement that practically nothing is known of the living of these animals and it is only by the reporting of the minutiae of such behavior as may be observed that we ever will know anything of them. Brief and scattered notes on the ways of life of these animals are available, but they are sometimes contradictory and always scant and quite insufficient to form a clear picture of this strange group.

The Aquarium mermaid was an immature Amazon manatee, *Trichechus inunguis* Natterer. It was a male, and while its overall length was about thirty-six inches and its weight about thirty pounds, we have no data at all on which to base an estimate of its age. It appeared to be quite young, though.

This species is rarely exhibited anywhere; a careful search of available notes and reports of the world's various zoological parks and aquaria indicated that not more than six or eight of them have ever been captured successfully and shown in places distant from their waters of origin. These consist of most of the fresh-water systems of northeastern South America, and in some parts of this area the animal is relatively abundant and is hunted by the natives as a source of meat and oil.

However, no manatee is particularly easy to catch alive, and for reasons which will be adduced later, they are difficult animals to transport and keep and, consequently, on which to assemble information.

The recent Aquarium manatee was caught and delivered to us by Paramount Aquarium, Inc., of New York, a firm of fish and animal collectors with stations all over the world.

We had requested this firm to procure a pair of these animals sometime ago, and word had been sent to all their stations in manatee country.

However, none had been forthcoming. Early this year, Mr. Marius Kramer, chief collector for the company, was starting on a tour of inspection of the Amazon stations and agreed to do what he could to catch our manatees for us. He knew that manatees were to be found up the Rio Tapajos, so when he arrived at Santarem, the base for this part of the country, he took Mr. Liebold, the station agent, and a collecting crew of natives up-stream. Distances in this part of the world are measured by days of travel and when they were about ten days up the Tapajos they found our recent exhibit leisurely coasting along the shores of a small lagoon. It was secured by use of a large seine.

Hunting for a mate for it was commenced immediately, but Mr. Kramer had contracted a number of tropical diseases on the way up stream, and suddenly took a turn for the worse so that it became imperative to rush him off to hospital, about eighteen days away in Belem (Para). On this miserable trip, Mr. Kramer insisted that the manatee be brought along and saw to it that the beast had all the care and attention it needed until he was able to turn it over to Mr. Hora, manager of the Para station, in whose care it could safely await shipment to New York.

In Belem the manatee was kept in one of the company's pools in the gardens of the botanical and zoological park while a shipment of fishes and animals was being assembled and awaiting the arrival of an ocean fish transporter. Eventually the beast, along with about one hundred thousand other creatures, mostly small fishes, was placed in the fish rooms of the Booth-Mallory steamer Crispin for passage to New York. Mr. Reinhold Hawer was the runner in charge of this shipment.

Mr. Hawer has a long and extensive experience handling animals of all sorts in all parts of the world, and while he knew little, from first hand, of the difficulties of transporting manatees, he has an excellent animal sense. Accordingly, he put the creature into a box approximately ten feet long by four wide by three deep, about three quarters filled with water. In such an excessively large box the little creature seemed lost, but there is an excellent reason for using so much water. These animals are mammals with a definite body temperature—almost one hundred degrees—to maintain. They live in water which constantly robs them of heat so that they are adapted to produce heat to compensate for this continuous loss. Consequently, if they are kept in a small quantity of water which is not continually changed, the water will become heated and perhaps "stew" the creature to death. We have no records of the amount of heat dissipated into water by a manatee, but we do have some records on porpoises, aquatic mammals which also never leave the water of their own volition as do seals and sea lions. In the case of porpoises we have found that an animal of medium size will raise the temperature of several hundred gallons of water twenty-five degrees in an hour. For this reason, then, Mr. Hawer provided the large box of water. Even so, he had to change and temper the fresh water several times a day—no light task at sea.

At the end of three weeks at sea, Mr. Hawer was exceedingly relieved to be able to turn the creature over to us, which he did on August 3, 1939.

All we had been able to learn of the diet of the manatee during its travels and stopovers was that it ate salad. This, in tropical countries and at sea, may mean anything, but usually includes lettuce, so that in spite of the tiny amount of definite information available about these manatees, we had at least one lead as to its diet. If it had lived for several months with lettuce, it would probably live for a little while with us on the same diet while we looked about for something else for it to eat. However, it was reported by Mr. Hawer that he had heard in Para that the beast had not yet been weaned. Mr. Kramer was incommunicado in hospital so no information was forthcoming from him. Mr. Hawer had not given it any milk aboard ship. Although we considered for a while the possibility of offering it milk, we decided that even if it had not been weaned when it was caught, it had suffered a drastic weaning after capture and there was no use returning it to a milk diet. Consequently, lettuce was the order of the day.

The manatee took this somewhat languidly and a hurry call for other vegetables and fruits was sent out. However, although most every kind of fruit and vegetable available through the market was tried, and such aquatic vegetation as we were able to collect ourselves, together with tropical lily pads, stalks, and blossoms kindly given to us by the Brooklyn Botanic Garden through the courtesy of Dr. George M. Reed, we found nothing that the beast would eat, save an occasional handful of an alga, Spirogyra. It would eat a little of this one day, but not the next, so we were still looking for foods other than lettuce at the time the creature died.

In all the reports we have read on the feeding of these beasts, we find unanimity in only one thing—bread. Manatees both free and captive are reported as eating bread freely, and one kept in this Aquarium twenty years ago ate one loaf of bread daily. However, this newest animal of ours was not interested in the least in the bread, which disappointed us, for we thought that the amount of lettuce it took each day was incompatible with the amount of energy it used, and bread is much more substantial than lettuce leaves.

However, in this respect our ideas may not be much good, for almost all of the Aquarium's charges are carnivorous and gulp down comparatively large quantities of concentrated proteins, while the manatee—all manatees are vegetarians—may extract much more nourishment from its rabbit food than we expect.

Some of the volunteer information we received following the pub-
licity attending the arrival of the creature at the Aquarium indicated that
(1) the manatee ate vegetation suspended above the water, (2) that the
manatee ate vegetation anchored at the bottom of the water, (3) that the
manatee ate vegetation floating at the surface. Since some of our visitors
had been stationed in manatee country and appeared to be competent
observers, we rigged up devices which would enable the creature to take
food at any of these levels. It took it from the surface of the water, although
it would occasionally root along the bottom. It would not reach above the
surface even when it was hungry. The amount of food the animal ate was
difficult to ascertain, for we followed the practice of keeping a plethora of
fresh green lettuce leaves in the tank. Many of the leaves were partly
chewed and then discarded, but we should estimate that between a
quarter and a half a bushel was eaten daily.

Something else puzzled us about the beast's dietary habits. When it
first arrived it appeared to be eating sand which it found at the bottom of
the tank. There are all sorts of theoretical reasons why such an animal
might eat sand, but none of them seemed to be quite valid, so top soil
mud was put into the tank as well as sand. Some of the mud was eaten
immediately, which seems to bear out what has been reported—that it
eats mud occasionally as an aid to elimination.

While we were looking for extra items of diet for the beast, we
observed from its faeces evidence that it was getting plenty of nourishment and was in no danger of actual starvation. The appropriate temperature at which the animal should be kept presented some problems.

Since it comes from the same waters as many of the small tropical
fishes kept as domestic pets, we considered that water suitable in temperature for them would be suitable for it. This is about 78 degrees
Farenheit. However, many reports we had gathered indicated that water
cooler than this was most suitable. Our voluntary aid detachment again
came to the fore in this respect and we were advised to keep the animal in
waters with temperatures ranging from forty degrees to ninety degrees.
What we did was to let the animal decide for itself which temperature it
liked. We did this by putting two streams of water into the tank, at
opposite corners, one running at seventy-eight degrees and the other at
sixty-eight degrees. Without hesitation the animal selected the higher
temperature. It was one of the few decisive things we ever saw it do.

However, even its decisiveness was alloyed on this score, for when
the colder water was sprayed into the tank as rain, the beast swam over
and "sat" under the cool rain. It did not remain there permanently, so the
temperature of the tank was kept at seventy-eight degrees, within a
degree or so one way or the other.

A further experiment was made to see if the manatee had any preference as to depth of water. The tank in which it lived, roughly eight feet
wide by eleven feet long, had about four feet of water in it. A sort of
platform of roughly-trimmed logs was built across the tank, rising from
the floor and reaching the surface of the water on the opposite side. The
angle was about 30 degrees and the idea was that if the beast had any
particular preference, it would indicate it by resting at the chosen level.
However, with the exception of two or three observations in more than
two weeks, it always floated free in the deepest part of the tank and
apparently did not care what the depth of water was. Toward the end of its
stay with us it seemed to use the logs more frequently, floating above
them and holding one between the tips of its flippers.

As a matter of fact, the manatee seemed to prefer the deep part of the
tank next to the glass front most of the day, which was fortunate for our
visitors, for without any forcing at all it stayed in full view of the spec-
tators practically all the time.

The general behavior of our mermaid was lackadaisical in the extreme. Its normal position somewhat resembled an angular parabola, if
there is such a thing, the head and tail being held downward in the water
with the back up. The comparatively enormous lungs filled with air
probably cause this position. Whether the manatee was floating at the
surface, resting on its flippers at the bottom, or floating midway between
bottom and top of the water, the posture of the body was the same except
when it made an effort to catch a bit of food floating at the surface or when
it was breathing.

The flippers were usually hanging limply downward, frequently
quite still and at other times with the smallest quiverings. This resembled
shivering and it was reported to us several times that the beast was
shivering with cold. It may have been shivering, although we doubt the
cold. We did find that if the beast floated without quivers it would be
carried along by the gentle current of water in the tank, whereas, when
the flippers quivered, the manatee remained in one position. The quiver-
ing, then, appeared to be some sort of minor locomotive effort. This is
exactly the same as the finning of fishes, a method of locomotion used to
maintain a definite position in respect to a fixed object and not in relation
to a flowing current of water, and shows how completely adapted to a
totally aquatic environment a mammal may become.

Long resting periods occurred throughout the day. They certainly
occurred during the night, but we did not find out if the beast actually
slept. The eyes were tiny, not more than one-eighth of an inch wide by
three-sixteenths long, and while they were shiny black, when one could
see them, it was usually impossible to note whether they were closed or

open at any time. We observed that the creature rose to breathe as frequently as four times in one minute when it was feeding. On one occasion during the night, it did not raise its head to breathe for a little longer than fourteen minutes. However, not more than two or three minutes elapsed between breaths during daylight hours, and between four and nine minutes during the night, as a rule. The fourteen-minute observation was made while the creature was floating about two feet below the surface and about one foot above the bottom of the tank, when it was hanging in mid-water as if suspended by a cord.

It was an extremely mild-mannered beast, taking food from our hands in less than two days after arrival. Its snout was soft, comparable to the lips of a horse, and if it sucked in a finger occasionally, it did not bite at all. It had no front teeth, but did have molars, the exact number being unascertainable in life. It is a matter of record that the number of these chewing teeth varies considerably. Apparently there is a constant supply of new ones coming from the back to take the place of old ones which are worn out.

The lips were flexible and equipped with a relatively heavy growth of bristles. These seemed to be used to help the lips work food into the mouth, which usually exposed a grayish mass of gum-like tissue.

The nostrils were large and at the top of the snout. They were marked by the grayish crescent at the edges of the flaps which were automatically closed while the creature was below water. When it breathed, these were pulled open, and if the creature was disturbed while breathing, and shut them quickly, a distinctly audible snap was heard.

The ears were not visible at all. They are reported as being nothing more than tiny slits at the best of times, but while it was alive we did not see even slits in our beast.

In general, the appearance of the creature was like nothing one could possibly imagine. The head was shaped roughly like that of a hippopotamus, the neck was non-existent, but there was a crease in the skin where the neck might be supposed to be. The body was somewhat egg-shaped, and not more than half as big again as the head. The tail was a flat paddle, more round at the end, and strongly ridged, with the edges turned downward. This paddle looked as if a strong rigid tail had been forced downward, the hind legs forced backward and upward, and a flattish rubber container slipped over all three members.

In color the beast was a dull, lead gray, sparsely bristled, and the general appearance as far from prepossessing as it well could be. It is difficult to conceive that this or any of its relatives could ever have possibly suggested a mermaid. Apologists for the mermaid myths tell us that if such an animal is viewed from a distance as it sits high out of the water

A ventral view (*top*) of a young male Amazonian manatee clearly displays the pink belly patch typical of the species. Note too the sharply defined phalanges at the end of the left flipper. The slightly smaller specimen (*bottom*) shows the contrasting darker dorsal surface. Photo courtesy of James Lovisek, Royal Ontario Museum, Toronto.

against the rays of the setting sun, the lines of the head flowing into those of the body may suggest flowing locks. The ineffectual scratchings of its head with the flippers may suggest combing of these same locks, and the lack of reflected light from the face prevents the features being distinguished. Consequently, the mermaid. However, not by any stretch of our imagination could we translate any of our manatee's activities, or its appearance, into those of a mermaid, or of any other kind of maid whatever.

Of course all such ideas are entirely subjective and it may be that other persons can imagine more vividly than we.

Our latest manatee died during the morning of August 25, twenty-two days after it was received. A thorough examination of the body was made by Mr. H. C. Raven, Prosector of the Society. His report indicates that the organs were in good condition; that the animal had been eating and was sufficiently fat; and that deep-seated ulcers found in the muscles of the back were the probable cause of death. There was no external manifestation of these ulcers, which were certainly not of recent origin. There was no trace of any foreign body in the necrotic area so that its cause is problematical. We are informed, however, that similar conditions are not uncommonly found in mammals taken wild.

Some quarter of a century after Coates wrote this description, in September 1967, Butterball, 3 feet 2½ inches and 63 pounds, arrived in San Francisco. He had been captured about a month earlier in the Amazon River near Leticia, Columbia, and was air-freighted via Florida to Earl S. Herald, who by then was director of Steinhart Aquarium in Golden Gate Park, the one-time home of Eugenie, the dugong mermaid.

The arrival of this immature male Amazonian manatee must have been a joyous occasion tempered with some apprehension. He suffered from a spear wound from which exuded malodorous pus reminiscent of the ill-fated Eugenie's wound. The puncture was packed with gauze and antibiotic ointment, and chloraphenicol was injected into the muscles. On his second day at Steinhart, Butterball was removed from his tank for radiography of the wound area. This clearly showed bone damage to three lumbar vertebrae but showed also areas where new bone was forming. Again the animal was medicated, then returned to his tank. Treatment continued for six and one-half months. Although the freshened wound edges were deeply sutured through the skin and tied over large buttons, the wound would not heal. Constant immersion in water was the problem, but how do you maintain an aquatic mammal out of its environment for weeks at a time? In air Butterball's thermoregulatory systems would be unable to function. The skin would dehydrate, peel, and crack in hideous convolutions. To keep the manatee as still as possible without damaging his natural functions, he was suspended for two and one-half weeks in a heavily padded nylon webb sling. Water jets delivered temperature-regulated sprays over his body, except for the wound area. Apparently unflustered by such indignities, Butterball daily consumed fifteen to twenty heads of lettuce. Finally, the sutures were removed, medication was discontinued, and he was returned to his environment. Another set of radiographs showed the bones had healed with no more than slightly depressed scars marking the healed areas.

Butterball had made it. Within a year of his arrival in San Francisco he had grown 24 inches (to 63 inches) and had gained 112 pounds (to 175). By the end of his second year, his lettuce consumption had reached a startling twenty-five heads a day; his weight was a bit over 227 pounds.

Rows of Amazonian manatees and Arapaima (*Arapaima gigas*) fish provide
ample food for residents of a Brazilian jungle village. Hunting to excess with
little thought of game management has led to the current endangered status of
T. inunguis. Photo from *National Geographic*, April 1926, © National Geographic
Society.

Other Amazonian (or Natterer's) manatees have been maintained in
captivity in zoos and aquariums of the world. In the United States,
records of the St. Louis Zoological Park show that three specimens have
been on display, two for no less than 10 years and the last as late as 1973.
Other individuals of the species are in captivity: in Higashi-Izu, Japan;
Manaus and Belem, Brazil; and Yomiuriland, Tokyo, Japan.

The Amazonian manatee apparently is confined to the Amazon Basin
and Orinoco River drainage. In Brazil it occurs in the Amazon and its
tributaries: Rios Tocantins, Xingu, Negro, Madeira; and the Tapajos and
Nhamunda. It has also been reported in the Rio Branco, which is almost
continuous with the Essequibo and Rupununi rivers of Guyana during
flooding, thus allowing manatees access to these rivers. Amazonian
manatees formerly were brought by the thousands to Manaus in western
Brazil for trade. The meat was more highly prized than beef. If not used
fresh or salted, it was boiled in its own fat in a preparation called *mixira* for

use at home as well as export abroad. In the interior, natives made shields of the hides. Thousands of the tough skins also were shipped to Rio de Janeiro or Portugal for manufacture into water hoses and machine belting.

Amazonian manatees also inhabit the upper Orinoco, Lake Maracaibo, and the sluggish tributaries of rivers of the plains of Venezuela. During the rainy season they are said to move into these flooded plains areas, where they are most vulnerable to hunters who take them for their meat and fat. Hides are made into whips and canes, and the bones, toasted and ground, are said to provide relief from asthma. In Colombia manatees live in the Amazon and in reaches of the Putumayo, Caqueta, and Apaporis rivers. In Peru they inhabit the Rios Napo, Rigre, Maranon, Samiria, and Pacaya, as well as the drainages of the Ucayli and Huallago.

Protective legislation has been enacted throughout the range of the Amazonian manatee. They are totally protected in Guyana, Brazil, Colombia, Venezuela, and Peru. This has helped regulate and reduce the rate of exploitation but, as one can well imagine, control in the inaccessible reaches of the interior is difficult, if not impossible. Add to this the threat of jaguars, caiman, piranha, and even the freshwater sharks of Lake Maracaibo, as well as pollution of that lake caused by farm land clearance, and it is simple to understand why the species may become extinct in the next few decades.

In July 1975, nearly eight years after Butterball's arrival at the California Academy of Sciences, my family and I paid him a visit. We waited in apparently endless lines of weekend visitors to the magnificent Steinhart Aquarium, and we waited again as, once inside, each visitor studied every aquarium, reducing traffic flow to a snail's pace. Impatiently, I forced my way through the throng to the large corner aquatic environment where I knew Butterball lived. Several family and school groups were crowded at the rail. Adults and teachers read graphic legends to the children, emphasizing important educational points. The groups blocked my view so that I was able to see only the upper half of the aquarium. There swam a large Tambique and a giant Arapaima, fishes from the rivers of South America that would be found in the freshwater manatee's normal habitat. The groups eventually moved on, and I slipped into the void at the rail. There he was, resting peacefully on the bottom, a picture of contentment among his friends from the wilds of Amazonia. Soon he lurched to the surface for a breath of air and displayed the pink belly patch unique to the species. He certainly lived up to his name; from his bristly muzzle to the circumference of his spatulate tail he was absolutely rotund.

Men of the upper Brazilian Amazon pose with their bounty. The hunt (c. 1970) was described to the author in the following manner: "The long-shafted harpoon bears a multibarbed detachable head that serves to secure the animal to the line. Being poor swimmers, the manatees quickly tire and surface for air whereupon the hunter manages to drive a wooden peg into one nostril. The enraged beast fights even more to a state of exhaustion and is forced to surface again. The second peg driven into the remaining nostril completes the job." Photos from Instituto Nacional de Pesquisas da Amazonia, Manaus, Brazil.

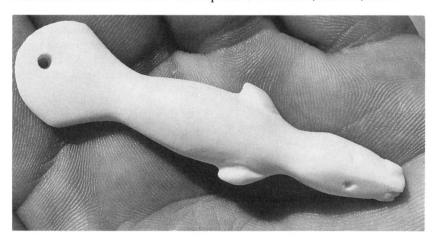

Numerous references to carved ivorylike manatee bone led to a search for photographs, sketches, or examples of such relics. The author was unable to locate a single specimen and was on the verge of considering the point no more than hypothesis when Diana Magor, based in Manaus, brought him this small amulet representation of an Amazonian manatee from Brazil. Photo courtesy of Miami Seaquarium.

At Steinhart Aquarium, Butterball is fed nothing but lettuce, usually about twenty-five heads a day. All food that goes into the tank is weighed, and what is not eaten is also weighed so that an exact record of food consumption is maintained. He is in a 1,300-gallon tank in the aquarium's heated freshwater system. The temperature is 82° F. Turnover rate for the entire system is about once every three and one-half hours. A one-inch portable filter cleans up bits of debris from the lettuce. In lieu of chemical additives, the water system has an ultraviolet sterilizer to control numbers of bacteria. Photo courtesy of Steinhart Aquarium, California Academy of Sciences, San Francisco.

Evenly spaced silky hairs covered his smooth brown hide. He looked like a milk-chocolate creation of the Candy Factory in San Francisco's Ghiardelli Square and obviously earned the affection of every passerby.

West African Manatee

Data on the West African manatee, *Trichechus senegalensis* (Link 1788), is sparse, and small wonder: they share their freshwater ecological niche with all manner of beasts dangerous to man. Coastal marine waters abound with voracious sharks. Crocodiles, hippos, and electric fishes tend to dampen a researcher's enthusiasm for field study. Add to this the highly secretive behavior of the West African manatee throughout its native haunts, and the chances for meaningful research narrow to less than attractive or even reasonable odds. Nonetheless, the unglamorous African manatee is a subject of modern scientific scrutiny. Facts are being gathered about where and when it moves, its social life, its nutritional requirements, and its population dynamics and taxonomy.

Taxonomic studies comparing the African manatee to the West Indian manatee (*T. manatus*) should prove of great interest. A certain few structural differences exist, but dugong species were highly similar even though their geographic ranges were widely separated, and one cannot help wondering if the same will prove true for these manatee species as well. In fact, the African and West Indian manatees are indistinguishable from the outside; this very similarity is taken as evidence to support the theory of continental drift, wherein tectonic plates are believed to have separated, leaving breeding individuals of a species on the isolated land masses. Other researchers feel that a number of the animals might simply have managed inadvertently to cross the water mass, thereby becoming established on both continents.

African manatees are found in many rivers and lagoons along coastal waters from Senegal to Angola. They have traveled far enough up rivers to have been noted a scant few hundred miles from that proverbial end of the earth, Timbuktu. Currently, they are protected in Senegal, Guinea, Sierra Leone, Liberia, Ivory Coast, Ghana, Togo, Dahomey, Nigeria, Gabon, Cameroon, Congo, Brazzaville, Zaire, and Angola.

The species was reported as rare in Senegal as early as 1800. As with other Sirenians, it is small wonder African manatees have been so seriously depleted. Many people of Africa feel that as a culinary dish, manatee meat has no equal. Rendered blubber is believed to have both prophylactic and curative properties, and certain body parts, the head and teeth in particular, are thought to confer powers in every imaginable field. Although against the law, heavy hunting of so useful a creature as "mammie-fish" (the manatee) continues. The hunter stands his silent watch at night on a platform constructed on the edge of deep water. Succulent grasses float on the surface, tethered by a line to a spot just in front of the harpooner. Slender wooden rods form a loose barricade on the deep-water side of the bait; the quarry moves and parts the rods as it moves in to feed upon the bait. The hunter strikes, sinking the barbed iron head of his harpoon deep into the back of the beast. The head detaches from the shaft and the mortally wounded animal thrashes away, towing a palm log float affixed by a line to the iron. The calls of the hunter

A male West African manatee, *Trichechus senegalensis* (Link, 1778), peers through crystalline water in his private pool at the Société Royal de Zoologie D'Anvers, safe from the rigors of his former home. His extended flipper clearly displays three heavy nails along its distal margin. These are found in West Indian manatees as well but are lacking in both Amazonian manatees and dugongs. Photos courtesy of Fundación para la Defensa de la Naturaleza (FUDENA).

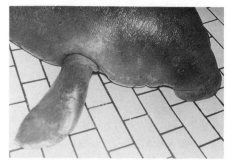

now summon others waiting nearby in a canoe, who follow the float and soon dispatch their prize and tow it ashore for butchering. Although hunting or sale of manatees or their parts or products is illegal, an entire animal will bring up to $800 on the underground market.

A multiplicity of other hazards threatens this beleaguered species. Waterway boat traffic takes its toll. In one area of Nigeria, the Ijaw fishermen considered the mammie-fish or water pig (both vernacular names for the manatee) such a hazard to navigation that, between 1932 and 1934, the animals were purposely eliminated. By means of an apparently highly efficient stockade trap, forty manatees were taken the first year, six the second, and none thereafter. The Anambr waterway system from which they were wiped out remains free of them to this day. Land runoff from expansion of farming areas, carrying with it residues from natural and chemical fertilizers and pesticides, will add to the water pig's depletion or at the very least will alter its range. The recently formed Lake Kainje in Nigeria and Lake Volta in Ghana rapidly are being choked with aquatic weeds. Herbicidal controls are in progress, but they too threaten the lives of vegetarian manatees living in the lakes, manatees that might one day afford a cost-free weed control

An engraving of the African man-
atee graces a postage stamp of the
Republic of Niger. Note the bottom
line, a plea for "Protection of Our
Fauna." Courtesy of Electa Pace,
Marine Films–Medifilms.

program. The resulting growth in commercial boat traffic will prove an insurmountable hazard, and the frustration will be complete; the same technology that provides refuges for the threatened species creates the means of destroying it. Humans seem unwilling at this time to coexist with aquatic mammals. As for the latter, perhaps their time on earth is nearing the end.

West Indian Manatees ≋

The peninsula of Florida is geologically young, and most of its topography was created by the flooding and receding of interglacial seas. Much of the land is so low in elevation that seawater and freshwater flowing from the land mingle throughout immense areas that fluctuate from salt to fresh with the tides. For centuries, access was so difficult that the subtropical wilderness remained untouched by man. Florida lies within the temperate zone but is strongly affected by the nearby Gulf Stream and by tropical trade winds. Rainfall may fluctuate from severe drought to more than 120 inches a year. Temperatures range from torrid highs to chilling winter frosts. These and a multitude of other factors make Florida a region of dynamic ecological variety, and possibly because of this variety, the last stronghold of the West Indian manatee (*Trichechus manatus* [Linne, 1758]) in the continental United States.

In times past, manatees ranged eastern American coastal waters from North Carolina southward around Florida (the Florida manatee subspecies) and among the islands of the Caribbean, along the coast of the Gulf of Mexico, to the eastern Atlantic bulge of Brazil (the Antillean manatee subspecies). Today, as with all other Sirenians, populations are greatly reduced almost in direct proportion to the development and advancement of civilization. Even the Florida peninsula supports only divergent relict populations.

As far back as 10,000 to 20,000 years ago, aboriginal man first penetrated this wilderness from the north. Ais, Apalachee, Timucuan, Jeaga, Calusa, and Tequesta tribes, all considered to have been of the same more northern origin, migrated to various areas of the Florida peninsula. The phenomenal variety of abundant plant and animal life provided amply for aboriginal needs. The Indians' refuse was cast in heaps, known today as middens. These ranged from fairly small mounds left by wandering groups to others of immense proportions; for example, one was found covering an area of 135 acres that rose in places to some 20 feet. Cross sections of these mounds reveal to anthropologists the ways of life of the tribes. Even those dating back to the period of earliest occupation of the peninsula contain remains of manatees. So docile a beast, in spite of its immense size, apparently posed little difficulty for the most primitive hunters, forced to stalk their prey from the water's edge. After about 5000 B.C. watercraft came into use and expanded the hunters' range. The oldest known dugout canoe in Florida has been radiocarbon dated at 1090 B.C. It had become an essential piece of hunting equipment and provided aboriginals with relatively easy access throughout their wilderness domain. By A.D. 1, they ranged throughout the peninsula.

In middens no weapons or tools designed specifically for manatee hunting have been found, but some remains prove that sea cows were hunted successfully to provide protein and fat for aboriginal diets. North Florida tribes would have found the beasts congregated in herds in the warm waters of thermal springs during chill winter weather. Archeological sites where manatee bones have been found are located for the most part along rivers with large thermal springs known to have supported winter populations of manatees in the past and even now—the Main Springs on the Suwannee River. Other sites exist along rivers not associated with springs—the Withlacoochee, Sante Fe, and Chipola. These contain sea cow bones and teeth fragments and bones of smaller animals as well as projectile points and tools. Such accumulations are thought to have been kill sites. They are located directly downstream from rapids where animals might be taken with comparative ease as they crossed the shallows. It would be reasonable to suggest that the aboriginal Floridians butchered and took what they wanted of the carcass at the kill site. The remains were left to become the accumulations found today.

In South Florida the Calusa and Tequesta tribes took manatees from time to time in rivers and along the coast. The Calusa developed a relatively complex social organization that was effective enough to cause the Spaniards to abort their first efforts to subdue them. The Indians were well armed with clubs, bows and arrows, and spears that were hurled with great force with the help of the *atlatl*, or spearthrower. With organization, reasonably efficient weapons, and aboriginal hunting skills they would have had little difficulty in killing even so wary a prey as the manatee. The Tequesta were skilled and daring hunters who in their canoes pursued marine turtles, sharks, rays, sailfish, porpoises, and especially the sea cows they considered a delicacy. Crude fiber ropes and wooden stakes served as harpoons. Clearly, the beasts were exploited as a food resource, but probably were not a staple diet item and suffered comparatively little hunting pressure.

In the Caribbean, off the coast of La Isla Española near the Rio de Oro, an early seafarer noted in the ship's log that three mermaids rose high out of the sea. He had seen them before off the African coast of Guinea. His notes apparently confirmed earlier thoughts that these were the legendary sirens, and certainly they were not as beautiful as they had been painted. The sighting of these creatures was the first written record by a European of manatees in the New World. La Isla Española is today Hispañola, that beautiful island shared by the Dominican Republic and Haiti. The year was A.D. 1493; the log was that of the intrepid little caravel, Niña; the seafarer was Christopher Columbus. During his fourth voyage in 1502, he saw them again. With Columbus was his young son, Ferdinand, who noted the sirens might "not be fishes but real calves . . . inside they have nothing like a fish." The boy also commented that they fed only on grass and that their meat looked and tasted like veal.

One common name given to those New World aquatic animals, for reasons made obvious by comments such as those of Ferdinand Columbus, is *sea cow*.

The name *manatee* is said to be derived from the Haitian *manati*, meaning "big beaver." Cannibalistic Carib Indians were reported by early explorers to refer to them as *manatine*. Others credit the common name as a reference to the Spanish word *manos*, meaning "hands," an allusion to the manual dexterity of the beasts' foreflippers. As the numbers of adventurers, explorers, and naturalists to coasts of the New World increased in the sixteenth century the written records of manatees grew. People of the Mayan culture hunted them with a harpoon affixed to rope and buoy. The impaled beast was pursued until exhausted or dead and then towed ashore for butchering. Father Gaspar de Carvajal noted that Maranon River natives in South America "were covered from head to feet with little shields made out of the skins of manatees and these were such that a crossbow would not pierce them." Others noted similar use made of the tough dried hide by Indians of Guiana and the Orinoco. The Guianese were said to bait their prey with plants that are particularly succulent to the manatee. As the animals cautiously raised their heads above water to feed, the Indians shot them with arrows. Others, such as the Waraos of Guiana and Miskito Indians of eastern Nicaragua, followed the Mayan technique of harpoon, line, and float, and they finished off the beast by crushing its skull with a club. South American Indians of the Rio Negro

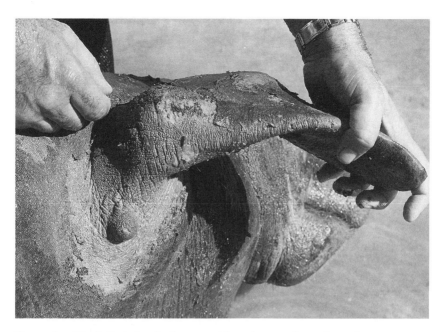

The author lifts Juliet's forelimb to provide a clear angle to show the mammary of a known lactating female. The abraded skin surface surrounding the nipple proves she is nursing a calf. Early New World explorers reported these animals as *manati* or *manatine*, names rooted in the old Carib Indian dialect meaning woman's breast. Photo courtesy of Miami Seaquarium.

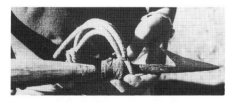

In the timeless jungle the Waraos and others still hunt *joninaba* (*joni*, river; *naba*, tapir; thus the river tapir) in the time-honored way with harpoons from hand-hewn dugouts. Photo courtesy of Eduardo Mondolfi, FUDENA.

"SAVE THE MANATEE" exclaims
the Wildlife Defense Fund poster
in Venezuela. Poster courtesy of
FUDENA.

and later the San Pedro fishermen of Mexico are said to have caught manatees with stout nets and dispatched them by driving wooden plugs into their nasal passages and suffocating them.

In 1516, as S.L. Peterson reports in her 1974 thesis on the manatee, an author described

> manatees and murene, and many other fishes which have no names in owre language . . . and not found I suppose in owre seas nor known to owre men before this tyme. This fish is four-footed, and in shape lyke unto a tortoise, although she be not couered with shel, but with scales; and those of such hardnesse and couched in such order, that no arrowe can hurte her. Her scales are byset and defend with a thousand knobbes. Her back is playne, and her heade utterly lyke the heade of an ox. She suyeth both in the water and on lande; she is slowe of mouing; of condition meeke, genteel, assocyable and louing to all mankind and of a marvelous sense of memorie as are the elephant and delphyn.
>
> There is a certain fish . . . named by the Indians as Iguaragua. . . . This fish is of an immense size. It feeds itself from herbs, as is indicated by

the chewed grama-grass which has been grasped in the bathed rocks of the mangrove-tree. . . . Close to its udders it has like two arms with which it swims; under the arms, udders with which it feeds its offsprings. It has a mouth totally similar to that of the ox. It is excellent to eat; you would not even know how to distinguish it as meat or first as fish. From its fat, which is inherent to its skin, and mainly towards the tail, brought to the fire, a sauce is made which can be compared to lard, and I do not know if it will surpass it. Its oil serves to season all foods: all its body is full of solid and very hard bones, such that at times can make ivory.

Peterson ascribes another account to a Portuguese seaman in 1601.

The eyes are exceedingly small for the body it hath, he shutteth and openeth them when he listeth . . . over the vents [nostrils] it hath two skins wherewith he closeth them, and by them he breatheth, and it cannot be long under without breathing, it hath no more nor other finnes but the taile; which is all round and close; the body is of a great bigness; all full of yellow haires, it hath two arms of a cubite long, with two hands round like peeles [stakes], and on them he hath fingers all close to one another, and on every finger he hath a nayle like a man's nayle. . . . The inward part and inwards of this fish are like an Oxes, with liver and lights, & c . . . The bones of this fish are massie [*sic*] and white like Ivorie.

Peterson goes on to quote other seventeenth-century reports:

The manatee . . . goes around salty water and in the rivers by the sweet water, which they drink. And they eat a tiny grass like millet that grows along the waterways. That fish has the same size of a two-year old calf and has two short limbs as arms, and they are fingerless hands; it does not have feet and has a tail like a cow. It has a very tender body, two gills and only one intestine. It has the liver and lungs, and most of the fat of an ox, and it is all very good. It does not have any scales, but a brownish and thick skin instead. These fish are killed with very big harpoons, attached to big and strong tail pieces; the end of it is attached to a barrel. Fishermen go in a jangada (a raft made of very light wood) following the barrel that the fish trails with him with madness until he bleeds to death, then floats, and the fishermen can take him to shore where they butcher the fish as they do with cows. The meat is very fat and tasty. His tail is like bacon, without any lean meat, which they melt as pork fat. It is used as butter that can be used like lard but with a better taste. The fish meat, cooked with vegetables, has the same taste as beef. It keeps the salt better, and, when seasoned, it looks and tastes like pork meat. If cured, it turns very red and it will taste as extremely good pork meat after cooked. . . . It has teeth like a cow and in the head, between the brain, it has a stone the size of a duck egg, made of three parts which are very white and hard as ivory. It has a great virtue against pain. The females have only one offspring and have sex like all other animals. The male has the testes and penus of an ox. The skin has no hair or scales.

In the "History of Animals and Trees of Maranhao" in 1632 by Friar Cristovao de Lisboa, which Peterson cites, the manatee is described as a "sea cow."

It has length from ten to twelve spans [the distance between the point of a man's thumb and tip of the little finger with the hand spread, generally accepted as nine inches] and the width of a cow; it is a dun-colored gray, has intestines and the haslet of a cow and nurses its offspring milk, and has its udders under its limbs. The male has, as its nature, the size of a horse and a peculiar shape, the tail is all fat, from which lard, good for frying, is made, and it is good for making hanging oil lamps. It has some size which gives ten or eleven arrobas [an arroba is about thirty-two pounds] and about six or seven jars of lard. Nothing is thrown out. Everything is eaten; even the tripes and the skin are good for cooking alone. They make shelter in the sea near the coast and in the month of March they go to the sweet water lakes and rivers to eat herbs and leaves. There would be a year in which three hundred fish or more would be killed. It has two rocks in its ear the size of a swollen button and it has two small ones attached to the large ones. The small ones serve for the air and the large ones serve for the ache of the rock [sic], something experimented in France. And I want to tell you what I saw happen to this fish: I saw a female get killed and skinned, and they threw the skin on the ground at the edge of the water. And the next day, going to get water, they found the offspring stretched out over the skin and they took it.

Although referred to as sea cow, ox-fish, and a multitude of other names, manatees conveniently were classified by the Roman Catholic church as a fish and could be consumed on days of religious abstinence (a parallel situation exists concerning dugongs and people of the Moslem faith). During the time of these sixteenth- and seventeenth-century writings the number of aboriginal Floridians was on the decline. Those not eliminated by disease, war, or enslavement departed with the Spaniards when the peninsula was surrendered to the British in 1763. As they left, whites, slaves, and Indians from the Carolinas, Georgia, and Alabama arrived in increasing numbers. Most of the Indians were settlers from the Creek Confederacy attracted by the unique land; they also were migrating southward as a result of pressure exerted by English settlements north of Florida. These Indians collectively became known as "Seminoles." Their economy was based on hunting, and they were not long in discovering the value of *E-chos-waw*, as they called the manatee in their native dialect.

Peterson reports an account of a visit to Manatee Springs in north central Florida in 1774:

> The basin and stream are continually peopled with prodigious numbers and variety of fish and other animals; as the alligator and manatee or sea cow, in the winter season; part of a skeleton of one which the Indians [Seminoles] had killed last winter, lay upon the banks of the spring; the grinding teeth were about an inch in diameter; the ribs eighteen inches in length, and two inches and an half thickness . . . this bone is esteemed equal to ivory; the flesh of this creature is found wholesome and pleasant food; the Indians call them by a name which signifies the big beaver.

The Florida Indian population probably numbered little more than 2,000 before the First Seminole War in 1813–14. The Indians lived primarily in the northern part of the peninsula. Following the Second Seminole War in 1835–47, most of them were forced to move to the Oklahoma Territory; possibly 500 remained, hidden in the southern watery wilderness known today as the Everglades. The Seminole and Miccosukee people quickly became masters of their semiaquatic domain. Their expertise with canoe and harpoon, and later with the rifle, helped them survive in this river of grass land that was far less hospitable than the forests of the north. They no longer enjoyed access to the thermal springs in and around which wildlife congregated and was taken with relative ease. Those who settled southern coasts managed with only a little more difficulty as noted in the following description of a hunt, reported by Peterson:

> Many of these animals are killed by the Indians every year. They hunt them in canoes, sometimes in the rivers, and again in the ocean, but usually near the mouth of the river. These animals come to the surface every few minutes to breathe and their heads may be seen as they appear for a moment above the surface of the water.
>
> They harpoon them as they rise to the surface using a steel point barbed on one side, attached to the end of a long pole. To the steel point is

fastened a strong cord, which in turn is attached to a float. Upon being struck the manatee sinks at once, but the direction in which he moves is indicated by the float. The Indians follow the float as closely as possible and watch for him to rise to the surface, when they shoot him through the head, and the huge animal is then towed to the shore. It requires considerable skill as well as strength to drive the harpoon through the thick, tough hide. Many of these animals grow to be very large size, and it is claimed that some of them have been taken which exceed twelve feet in length.

From the time of their first migrations into Florida, the Indians cared little for contact with other people. They did trade with colonists, wayfarers, and even buccaneers, and manatee meat, oil, and hides played a small role in these exchanges. However, news of this delicacy spread, and hunting expeditions from as far away as Europe were sent to the Americas. No one knows or has proposed estimates of what the sea cow population might have been at that time. Various authors began to report the bitter fact that where manatees had once been relatively abundant, now they were few or no longer existed at all. Obviously their numbers were in dismal decline.

As early as 1879, Peterson reports, observers in Florida began lamenting human encroachment upon the environment:

> But before many years shall pass away the scene will change. Civilization is encroaching; the restless settler is every year pushing farther and farther into the unknown wilds of Florida, and even now men are casting ahead to secure a homestead or to commence a speculation in some way on the lands or products of this region. Then it will surely happen that the peace-loving manatee will be driven away and they will become but a legend or old man's tale.
>
> The last two generations have witnessed such a destruction of animal life in this century that it is appalling to look ahead and see what the future has in store for us. . . .
>
> It is now eight years since he saw a living manatee, but when he first came to the river fifteen years ago they were still common and he often saw them from the door of his little house at the Narrows passing up and down the river and occasionally he saw them at play when they would roll up, one behind the other like coils of a great sea serpent.

By 1885 an observer wrote that "ten years ago the meat could be bought at fifty cents a pound. Of course the animals are becoming far too scarce to admit of its being sold at all. There is no doubt that the manatee is fast becoming an extinct animal. . . . The sea cow will pass out of existence . . . and the only remaining trace of its former existence will be a few old bones."

No more than a dozen years before these anxious observations were made, curiosity about manatees had triggered attempts to maintain them in artificial environments. Early recorded efforts include one animal housed in the Central Park menagerie in New York City in 1873.

In 1878, a large adult female manatee, which had arrived in Greencock, England in healthy condition, was purchased and immediately transferred to its final quarters in the Royal Westminster Aquarium in London. The animal had been taken in a net near the mouth of the Essiquibo River, British Guiana and was said to have been the only one observed in that locality for three years, thus yielding evidence of their grown [sic] scarcity. Native fishermen took it across at Demerara, and there it was bought on speculation by Captain Picott of the S.S. Blenheim, who, by the same evenings mail, dispatched a letter to the Managers of the Aquarium. On the voyage across the Atlantic, the large box containing the manatee was kept about two-thirds full of fresh water, and being placed near the donkey engine, steam was passed at intervals into the water so as to keep the latter up to a warm temperature. As the colder latitudes were reached, some trouble was taken to retain the water at a uniform heat. Before starting, a quantity of the fresh so-called "Moca-moca" leaves and fruit was obtained, which the creature devoured in a few days, and then it was supplied with liberal allowances of hay and a slight amount of bread. There is, however, no very conclusive evidence of its having consumed the latter.

On arriving at Greencock, the manatee was there bought by Mr. Carrington for the sum of £200, and the steamer proceeding onward, conveyed it to Glasgow. Here the tank was carted to St. Enoch's Station, Midland Railway, and dispatched in a covered car to London. Telegrams were sent to six different stations in advance to have a dozen or so buckets of hot water ready at each when the train arrived; the warm water was poured into the tank and the temperature thus kept up. Mr. Carrington himself sat alongside the tank all the journey by rail and during the night the manatee frequently raised itself, endeavoring to get out of the box. Whether the unusual sensation of railway traveling disturbed it, whether the chilling of the water and colder atmosphere of midnight affected it, or whether, evening being its natural active period caused the uneasiness, is uncertain. The strange traveling sensation, disturbance and rude shakings may have had their influences, for on first introduction into the Aquarium glass tank and for nearly a week after the manatee would not feed, stimulating concerns for her survival. Failing to observe cessation of its sulky humor or illness, as the case might be, and justly believing food a necessity, (on Mr. Carrington consulting me) I suggested the introduction of milk into its mouth by syringe. Accordingly, the water was drained off, and three persons entering the tank and inserting a cork in the fore part of the mouth, a small quantity of milk was several times given forcibly by syringe. The manatee, though ordinarily exceedingly quiet and gentle in its demeanor, evidently seriously objected to being thus unnaturally fed. Obliged to swallow a certain quantity of the milk and castor oil, it nevertheless rejected what it could, while displaying an astonishing force of body, tail and limbs. So great was its power that the three persons found the greatest difficulty in restraining its movements, and introducing the food. During this rough manipulation, and, indeed, during the whole of its after confinement in the tank, it was never heard to utter any sound indicative of voice; nor did it then, or even after, attempt to bite or otherwise injure those handling it, though, of course, with floundering, wriggling struggle, endeavouring to free itself from the grasp of its would-be friends. Whether its ailment had passed, the spirit of resistance had overcome the sulks, or it deemed feeding itself preferable to milk diet against its will, a very few days more elapsed when, to Mr. Carrington's satisfaction, it began spontaneously to munch and swallow the green food floating in the water. Thenceforward, its appetite improved; and by degrees it daily devoured astonishing quantities of vegetable stuffs, passed faeces naturally, and in all respects throve amazingly.

On first arrival at the Aquarium, cabbage, lettuce, watercress, pieces of carrot and turnip, loose and bundles of hay, and quantities of pondweed were put into the tank, both floating and sunk by weights attached. Occasionally it would sniff or examine these by snout and lips without chewing or swallowing, until its appetite returned as above mentioned. It then showed preference to watercress, though after taking cabbage; but afterwards it chose lettuce, and entirely eschewed the others. When in the height of health it consumed, according to Mr. Carrington, from 90 to 112 lbs of green food daily. As lettuce became scarce and dear, it cost 10s. a day to supply it with the French sort; and although cabbage &c. was then cheap and abundant, it daintily chose the former, and as steadily avoided and refused the latter.

For six months all went well, and numerous visitors came and went without disturbing the equanimity or destroying the appetite of this Sirenian. The tank water was kept at about 70° to 74° Fahr by steam being introduced at regular intervals or whenever the thermometer showed a depression. But just at Christmas time, during very cold weather, by accident the keeper one night in the dark unskillfully let the wasteplug loose or obliquely placed it in the hole; consequently, the water slowly drained away, and Manatee was left high and dry to suffer from a serious chill of the cold atmosphere. Next morning, when the water was run into the tank it showed signs of depression and illness, and thenceforth, apparently refusing all food, it daily became thinner and thinner, but lingered on until the 15th of March, 1879, when it died of sheer exhaustion.

Two West Indian manatees were exhibited in Key West, Florida, in 1880. A male was shipped to the New York Zoological Society in 1903 and was placed on public display for five months at the old New York Aquarium at the Battery. Another was captured in 1911 in Laguna Madre near Port Isabel, Texas, and was exhibited in New Orleans for at least half a year. Others captured in the same locale were sent to Houston and Chicago. In 1919, fishermen netted a manatee in Masonboro Sound near Wilmington, North Carolina. The beast was displayed in a lakeside enclosure until it died after a month or so, during a November cold spell. Three West Indian manatees were held and studied in the Bayfront Park Miami Aquarium in 1922. From there, fifteen years later, came the first description of the birth of a manatee by a female that had conceived in the wild. A second birth from a dam who had conceived in the wild was recorded in 1946 in a saltwater pool at the Theater of the Sea on Windley Key, Monroe County, Florida. The mother, who had survived at the attraction for about seven months, died when the calf was about five months old. The longevity record to date for a captive-born manatee conceived in the wild is held by the South Florida Museum in Bradenton: Baby Snoots has been pleasing visitors there since its birth on July 21, 1948; he still is going strong in 1992. Another manatee was born in 1955 at the Tropical Panorama Exhibit in Ojus, Florida, of a dam that had been captured several weeks before; the dam was lost a number of months thereafter, and the death of the baby was unrecorded.

Epilogue ❧

Steller's sea cow, *Hydrodamalis gigas*, is extinct. Humankind managed to wipe out the relict population of possibly 2,000 of these giants in just under 30 years in the late 1700s; twentieth-century technology must be far more efficient. Numbers of dugongs (*Dugong dugon*) throughout their Indo-Pacific marine range are not endangered in the current sense of the word, but they have diminished in many areas and today are absent in others where once they were known, even abundant. *Trichechus innunguis*, the Amazonian manatee, has been referred to as the most endangered Sirenian owing to its remote habitat and to relentless human pressures upon the population. The West African manatee, *T. senegalensis*, is diminishing in numbers, but so little is known about them that definitive statements are impossible at this time. The West Indian manatee, *T. manatus*, recently has been the subject of intense scrutiny; it should be, with only an estimated 14,000 remaining in its total range. Of these, 1,800 or less of the Florida manatee subspecies (*T.m. latirostris*) survive within U.S. waters, and those only in coastal waters from Texas through Florida. Without doubt the sea cow is the most endangered of aquatic mammals.

Political and technical conservation efforts currently range from legislation and sanctuaries to propeller guards and flood-control-gate protective equipment. But no measures will accomplish more than will public awareness of the plight of the manatee. Destroying or saving 60 million years of evolution is in our hands.

We have named Lorelei's son (Juliet's grandson) "Hugh."

Appendixes ≋

A. Cenozoic Era Geologic Distribution of Principal Genera of Sirenia
Diversification of mammals and birds; appearance of modern species and man.

FAMILY / GENUS	EOCENE (Began 54 million yrs. ago)			OLIGOCENE (Began 37 million yrs. ago)			MIOCENE (Began 25 million yrs. ago)			PLIOCENE (Began 10 million yrs. ago)			PLEISTOCENE (Began 2 million yrs. ago)	RECENT
	Lower	Middle	Upper	Lower	Middle	Upper	Lower	Middle	Upper	Lower	Middle	Upper		
PRORASTOMIDAE														
Porastomus		Jamaica												
PROTOSIRENIDAE														
Protosiren	Egypt													
DUGONGIDAE														
Eotheroides			N. Africa & Europe											
Prototherium			Italy											
Halitherium														
Caribosiren				Caribbean — Puerto Rico										
Anomotherium					Europe									
Rytiodus					Madagascar									
Metaxytherium					Germany — France		S. Amer. — Europe & N. Amer.							
Hesperosiren							N. Amer.							
Thalattosiren							Australia							
Prohalicore							France							
Miosiren							Belgium							
Hydrodamalis									N. Pacific ————————————— →					
Dugong														Indopacific
TRICHECHIDAE														
Sirenotherium						Brazil								
Potamosiren								Colombia						
Ribodon										Argentina			N. Amer.	
Trichechus													N. Amer.	S. Amer. & W. Africa

Source: Daryl P. Domning, Howard University, Washington, D.C.

B. Classification and Ranges of Recent Sirenians ≈

Phylum: Chordata

Class: Mammalia

Superorder: Paenungulata

Order: Sirenia

Family: Dugongidae—Artic Sea Cows and Dugongs.
Hydrodamalis gigas (Zimmerman, 1780)—Steller's Sea Cow. Marine; Bering Sea (recorded modern range 1742–68); extinct.

Dugong dugon (Muller, 1776)—Dugong.
Marine; Red Sea, Bay of Bengal, Malay Archipelago, Moluccas to Philippines, southward to New Guinea and northern Australia.

Family: Trichechidae—Manatees.
Trichechus inunguis (Natterer, 1883)—Amazonian manatee. Fresh water; Orinoco and Amazon river drainages of northern South America.

Trichechus senegalensis (Link, 1778)—West African manatee. Euryhaline; coastal and river drainages from Senegal River south to Cuanaga River, including Lake Chad drainage.

Trichechus manatus (Linné, 1758)—West Indian manatee. Represented by two subspecies: the Florida Manatee, *T. m. latirostris*, euryhaline, from Jacksonville, Florida, south discontinuously around peninsular Florida, coast occasionally in Florida Keys, west through Texas; Antillean manatee, *T. m. manatus*, euryhaline, coastal Central and South America to Brazil, West Indies, and Puerto Rico.

C. Legislation and Protection ≈

The manatee has been protected by Florida state law (Ch. 4208.94) since 1893, and in May 1907 (Ch. 370.12) the state imposed a fine of up to $500 and/or six months' imprisonment for killing or molesting a manatee. The 1907 statute was amended in 1953 to allow capture of manatees for scientific or educational purposes.

The Florida Manatee Sanctuary Act of 1978 further amended the 1907 state law by declaring the entire state of Florida a "refuge and sanctuary for the manatee." The act has been in effect since July 1, 1978, and provides for regulating boat speeds in 13 manatee aggregation areas between November 15 and March 31. Between 650 and 850 manatees are found around these 13 areas during the winter months.

State responsibility for manatee protection is vested with the Department of Natural Resources (DNR) and Florida Game and Fresh Water Fish Commission. Blue Spring State Park (a winter congregation area) was designated a manatee sanctuary by DNR in 1973. It was the first place in Florida where boats were prohibited and swimming was restricted specifically for manatee protection. The St. Johns River, 0.5 miles south and 0.37 miles north of the entrance to the run, has been posted by the state as a manatee refuge area with idle speed, no wake.

Federal efforts toward manatee protection began on March 11, 1967, when the manatee was listed as an endangered species under the Endangered Species Preservation Act of 1966 (P.L. 89-669; 80 Stat. 926). This act covered species in the United States and authorized acquisition of habitat but left protection to the states. The Endangered Species Conservation Act of 1969 (P.L. 91-135; 83 Stat. 275) superseded the 1966 act, and the manatee was listed again on December 2, 1970. The 1969 act regulated importation of listed species and extended its scope to cover species worldwide.

The Marine Mammal Protection Act (MMPA) of 1972 (P.L. 92-522; 80 Stat. 1027) established a national policy to protect and encourage the development of marine mammals to optimum sustainable population levels consistent with the maintenance of the health and stability of the ecosystem. The manatee was designated as a marine mammal under this act. State jurisdiction for marine mammals was preempted by the MMPA, and the jurisdiction over manatees was vested in the Department of the Interior, pending return of the management to states when their laws and regulations are found to be consistent with the act. The act prohibits taking any marine mammal. Violators of the act may be fined up to $20,000 and/or one year in prison.

The Endangered Species Act of 1973 (P.L. 94-359; 90 Stat. 913) super-seded the 1969 act and increased federal protection of manatees. The 1973 act made it a violation to harass, harm, pursue, hunt, shoot, wound, kill, capture, or collect endangered species. Violators of the act may be fined up to $20,000 and/or one year in prison. In addition, endangered species or parts or products may not be imported or exported. Exceptions may be made for "scientific purposes or to enhance the propagation or survival" of the species. The act also authorized cooperative agreements between states and the federal government with funding (1/3 state and 2/3 federal) for management, research, and law enforcement. A cooperative agree-ment between the U.S. Fish and Wildlife Service and the State of Florida on endangered species became effective on June 23, 1976. A similar agreement with the State of Georgia became effective on October 6, 1977. Applications have been made by the Florida DNR for federal funds for law enforcement and an information and education program on manatees.

A Florida Manatee Recovery Plan was first approved in 1980. A completed revision of the plan was approved in 1989. (Copies are available from the Fish and Wildlife Reference Service, 5430 Grosvenor Lane, Suite 110, Bethesda, MD 20814.) The plan was prepared by the Florida Manatee Recovery Team to "delineate reasonable actions believed required to place the assigned species in the best possible position for recovery. It is in-tended to serve as a guide that delineates and schedules those actions be-lieved necessary to restore the Florida manatee as a viable self-sustaining element of its ecosystem." The challenge of recovering the population of manatees is mind-boggling but certainly not impossible. It will take well-coordinated efforts of all local, state, and federal agencies; the rescue teams of Sea World of Florida, Miami Seaquarium, Disney's Living Seas at Epcot Center, Disney World, Lowry Park Zoo, and Homosassa Springs Nature World; groups such as Save the Manatee Club and Audubon; businesses such as Florida Power & Light and the Marine Industries Association of Florida; popular public personalities like the hardworking

Jimmy Buffett; and private citizens. Many of the tasks described in the recovery plan are well under way. An interim objective is to downlist Florida manatees from "endangered" to "threatened" pursuant to provisions of the Endangered Species Act of 1973. The long-range recovery goal, as required by the Marine Mammal Protection Act of 1972, is to maintain the "health and stability of the marine ecosystem" and to maintain numbers at "optimum sustainable population" levels in the southeastern United States.

A separate recovery plan has been prepared for the Antillean manatee in Puerto Rico.

D. Florida Refuges ≋

Natural and artificial warm-weather refuges are used by Florida manatees (*Trichechus manatus latirostris*); regulated areas are those in which operation and speed of motorboats will be regulated in Florida waters from November 15 to March 31 annually.

Natural warm-weather areas:

A. Welaka Spring
B. Silver Glen Spring Run
C. Blue Spring Run (regulated area, including connecting waters of St. Johns River)
D. Headwaters of Homosassa River (regulated area)
E. Headwaters of Crystal River (regulated area)
F. Manatee Springs

Artificial warm-water areas:

1. Alton Box Factory, Jacksonville
2. John D. Kennedy Generating Station, Jacksonville
3. Southside Generating Plant, Jacksonville
4. East Palatka Plant, East Palatka
5. Turner Generating Plant, Enterprise
6. Sanford Plant, DeBarry
7. Indian River Plant, Delespine (regulated area, Delespine and Frontenac power plants effluent; Indian River from St. Lucie Inlet to Jupiter Inlet)
8. Cape Kennedy Plant, Titusville
9. Vero Beach Municipal Power Plant, Vero Beach (regulated area, discharge canals and connecting waters)
10. Henry D. King Municipal Electric Station, Fort Pierce (regulated area, discharge canals and connecting waters)
11. Riviera Plant, Riviera Beach (regulated area, discharge canal and connecting waters)
12. Port Everglades Plant, Fort Lauderdale (regulated area)
13. Fort Lauderdale Plant, Fort Lauderdale (regulated area)

14. Miami River Plant, Miami
15. Turkey Point Generating Plant, Florida City
16. Fort Myers Plant, Tice (regulated area, Orange River and adjoining waters of the Caloosahatchee River)
17. Big Bend Generating Plant, Apollo Beach (regulated area, the Alafia River from Tampa Bay to U.S. 41)
18. Phosphate Plant, Gibsonton
19. Crystal River Plant, Crystal River

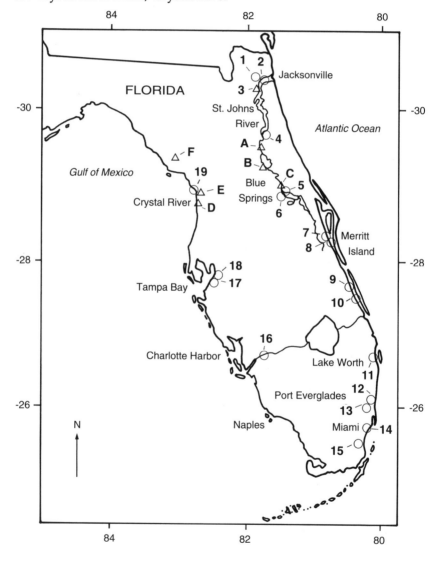

Bibliography ❊

Adams, M.P. Greenwood
1924. Australia's Wild Wonderland. *National Geographic* 45 (3): 329–56.
Allen, T.B.
1974. *Vanishing Wildlife of North America.* Washington, D.C.: National Geographic Society.
Allsopp, W.H.L.
1960. The Manatee: Ecology and Use for Weed Control. *Nature* (London) 188 (4752): 762.
Anderson, P.K.
1984. Suckling in *Dugong dugon. J. Mammal.* 65 (3): 510–11.
1986. Dugongs of Shark Bay, Australia: Seasonal Migration, Water Temperatures, and Forage. *National Geographic Res.* 2 (4): 473–90.
Asper, E.D.
1979. Commitment to Manatee Health, Research; Sea World's Role. *Fla. Conserv. News* 15 (2): 14–17.
Bachman, K.C., and A.B. Irvine
1978. Composition of Milk from a Florida Manatee, *Trichechus manatus latirostris. Comp. Biochem. Physiol.* 62A: 873–78.
Baker, G.S.
1980. How Much Do You Know on *Trichechus manatus? Fla. Conserv. News* 15 (6): 10–11.
Bertram, C., and G. Bertram
1966a. The Sirenia: A Vanishing Order of Animals. *Animal Kingdom* 69: 180–84.
1966b. The Dugong. *Nature* 209: 938–39.
1970a. The Dugongs of Ceylon. *Loris* 12 (1): 53–55.
1970b. Dugongs in Ceylon. *Oryx* (London) 10 (6): 362–64.
1971. The Decline of the Dugong. *Australian Nat. Hist.* 17 (4): 146–47.
1973. The Modern Sirenia: Their Distribution and Status. *Biol. J. Linn. Soc.* 5 (4): 297–338.
Bertram, C., and K. Bertram
1966a. Sea Cows Could Be Useful. *Sea Frontiers* 12 (4): 210–17.
1966b. Dugongs in Australian Waters. *Oryx* 8 (4): 221–22.

Bertram, G.
1943. Note on the Sea Cow in the Gulf of Aqaba. *Oryx* 47: 21–23.
Bertram, G., and C. Bertram
1962. Manatees of Guiana. *Nature* (London) 196 (4861): 1329.
1963. The Status of Manatees in the Guianas. *Oryx* 7 (2/3): 90–93.
1964. Manatees in the Guianas. *Zoologica* (N.Y.) 49 (6): 115–20.
1966. The Dugong. *Nature* (London) 209 (5026): 938–39.
1968. Bionomics of Dugongs and Manatees (*Hydrodamalis, Trichechus*). *Nature* (London) 128 (5140): 423–26.
Best, R.C.
1979a. Foods and Feeding Habits of Wild and Captive Sirenia. Instituto Nacional de Pesquisas da Amazonia, Manaus, Amazonas, Brazil.
1979b. Preliminary Report on the Distribution and Apparent Status of Manatees (Mammal: Sirenia) on the Northern Coast of Brazil. 8pp. Typescript.
1981. Foods and Feeding Habits of Wild and Captive Sirenia. *Mammal Review* 11 (1): 3–29.
Best, R.C., and G.J. Gallivan
1978. The West Indian Manatee (*Trichechus manatus*) in Brazil: A Survey to Determine Its Status and Present Distribution. 29pp. Proposal submitted to IUCN/WWF.
Best, R.C., and William E. Magnusson.
1979. Status Report of the Brazilian Manatee Project 1975–79, Instituto Nacional de Pesquisas da Amazonia, Manaus, Amazonas, Brazil.
Best, R.C., and V.M.F. da Silva
1979. O Peixe-boi: Uma Sereia na Represa? *CESPAULISTA* (Sao Paulo) 3 (16): 26–29.
Best, R.C.; S.P. dos Santos; W. Rodrigues; and D.M. Teixeira
1978. Avaliacao e Discriminacao de um Parque Nacional no Litoral do Territorio Federal do Amapa. 30pp. Typescript.
Buergelt, C.D.; R.K. Bonde; C.A. Beck; and T.J. O'Shea.
1984. Pathologic Findings in Manatees in Florida. *J. Amer. Vet. Med.* 185 (11): 1331–34.
Bullen, Ripley P., and H.K. Brooks
1967. Two Ancient Florida Dugout Canoes. *Quarterly J. Fla. Acad. of Sci.* 30 (2): 97–107.
Campbell, H.W.
1976. The Florida Manatee and Related Species. *Plaster Jacket* (Florida State Museum) 25.
1976. Endangered Species: The Manatee. *Fla. Naturalist* 15–20.
Campbell, H.W., and A.B. Irvine
1977. Feeding and Ecology of the West Indian Manatee, *Trichechus manatus* Linnaeus. *Aquaculture* 12: 249–51.

Nov. 1980. Commitment to Manatee Health, Research; The Laboratory's Role. *Fla. Conserv. News* 15 (2): 18–19.

Campbell, H.W.; A.B. Irvine; and D.K. Odell

1977. Winter 1977: Impact on Florida Manatees. Abstracts, 1977 Annual Meeting, Amer. Soc. of Mammal., no. 13.

Carr, Archie

1973. *The Everglades. The American Wilderness.* New York: Time.

1976. Operation Mermaid. *International Wildlife* 6 (2): 12–17.

Carvajal, Gaspar de

1934. *The Discovery of the Amazon According to the Account of Friar Gaspar de Carvajal and Other Documents, as Published with an Introduction by José T. Medina.* Translated by Bertram T. Lee. Edited by H.C. Heaton. New York: American Geographical Society.

Carvalho, J.C. de M.

1967. A conservacao da Natureza e Recursos Naturais na Amazonia Brasileira. *Atas Simp. Biota Amazônica* 7: 1–47.

Caton, Albert

July 1979. Dugong, Like Mermaids, Are Scarce but Northern Australian Population May Be Increasing. *Australian Fisheries.* Reprint no. 65.

Coates, C.

1939. Baby Mermaid—A Manatee At The Aquarium. *Bull. N.Y. Zool. Soc.* 42 (5): 140–48.

1940. Manatees at the Aquarium. *Bull. N.Y. Zool. Soc.* 43 (3): 99–100.

Crane, A.

1881. Notes on the Habits of the Manatees (*Manatus australis*) in Captivity in the Brighton Aquarium. *Proc. Zool. Soc.* (London) 1881: 456–60.

Cunningham, R.C.

1870. Concerning a Specimen of the Manatee (*M. americanus*) Kept Alive in Captivity. *Proc. Zool. Soc.* (London) 1870: 789.

Cushing, Frank H.

1897. Exploration of Ancient Key Dwellers' Remains on the Gulf Coast of Florida. *Proc. Amer. Philos. Soc.* 35 (153): 329–432.

Dekker, D.

1977. Birth of the Sea Cow: A Unique Event. *Artis* (Amsterdam) 23 (4): 111–19. English edition.

1980. Pre- and Postnatal Behavior in the Manatee (*Trichechus manatus*) in Captivity. *Aquatic Mammalogy* 8 (1): 21–26.

Domning, D.P.

1970. Sirenian Evolution in the North Pacific and the Origin of the Steller's Sea Cow. *Proc. Seventh Ann. Conf. Biol. Sonar Diving Mamm.* 7: 217–20.

1972. Steller's Sea Cow and the Origin of the North Pacific Aboriginal Whaling. *Syesis* 5: 187–89.

1977. Observations on the Myology of *Dugong dugon* (Müller). *Smithsonian*

Contributions to Zoology, no. 226. Washington, D.C.: Smithsonian Institution Press.

1978a. The Myology of the Amazonian Manatee, *Trichechus inunguis,* (Naterer) (Mammalia: Sirenia). *Acta Amazonica* 7 (2): 1–81.

1978b. Sirenia. Reprinted from *Evolution of African Mammals,* ed. Vincent J. Maglio and H.B.C. Cooke. Cambridge, Mass.: Harvard Univ. Press.

1981. Distribution and Status of Manatees, Trichechus SPP, Near the Mouth of the Amazon River, Brazil. *Biol. Conserv.* 19 (2): 85–97.

1982. Evolution of Manatees; A Speculative History. *J. Paleontology* 56 (3): 599–619.

1983. Marching Teeth of the Manatee. *Natural History* 92 (5): 8–11.

Domning, D.P., and L.C. Hayek

1984. Horizontal Tooth Replacement in the Amazonian Manatee (*Trichechus inunguis*). *Mammalia* 48 (1): 105–28.

Domning, D.P., and D. Magor

1977. Rate of Horizontal Tooth Replacement in Manatees. *Acta Amazonica* 7 (3): 435–38.

Farmer, Roy; Roy E. Weber; Joseph Bonaventura; Robin Best; and Daryl Domning

Functional Properties of Hemoglobin and Whole Blood in an Aquatic Mammal, the Amazonian Manatee (*Trichechus inunguis*). *Comp. Biochem. Physiol.* 62A: 231–38.

Gallo-Reynoso, J.P.

1983. Notes on the Distribution of the Manatee (*Trichechus manatus*) on the Coasts of Quintana Roo. *An. Inst. Biol. Univ. Nac. Auton.* (Mex. Ser. Zool.): 53 (1): 443–48.

Harry, R.R.

1956. Eugenie the Dugong Mermaid. *Pac. Discovery* 9 (1): 21.

Hartman, D.S.

1968. The Status of the Florida Manatee in Captivity. *Fla. Bd. Conserv. Div. Salt Water Fish.* 22pp.

1969. Florida's Manatees, Mermaids in Peril. *National Geographic* 136 (3): 342–53.

1970. Sea Nymphs and Elephants. Not Man Apart. Special wildlife issue published for Friends of the Environment, League of Conserv. Voters, 2 (2).

1971a. Observations of the American Manatee at Blue Springs Park, Volusia County, Florida, with notes on the species' current status and distribution in the Upper St. Johns River. 19pp. Unpublished report.

1971b. Behavior and Ecology of the Florida Manatee, *Trichechus manatus latirostris* (Harlan), at Crystal River, Citrus County. Ph.D. diss., Cornell Univ., Ithaca, N.Y.

1972. Manatees. *Sierra Club Bull.* 57 (3): 20–22.

1973a. Distribution and Status of the Manatee (*Trichechus manatus* Linnaeus) in the United States. 16pp. Manuscript.

1973b. Manatees Status Little Changed in 50 Years. World Wildlife Fund progress report, Fall 1973.

1979. Ecology and Behavior of the Manatee (*Trichechus manatus*) in Florida. Spec. Publ. no. 5. Amer. Soc. of Mammal., Pittsburgh, Pa. 142pp.

Heinsohn, G.E.

1976. W4—Sirenians—a draft report. Bergen Consultation ACMRR/RR/SC/WG 4–1. Bergen, Norway.

Heinsohn, G.E., and W.R. Birch

1972. Foods and Feeding Habits of the Dugong, *Dugong dugon* (Erxleben), in Northern Queensland, Australia. *Mammalia* 36 (3): 414–22.

Heinsohn, G.E., and A.V. Spain

1974. Effects of a Tropical Cyclone on Littoral and Sublittoral Communities and on a Population of Dugongs (*Dugong dugon*) (Müller). *Biol. Conserv.* 6 (2): 143–52.

Herald, E.

1969. Aquatic Mammals at Steinhart Aquarium. *Pac. Discovery* 22 (6): 26–30.

Hoenstine, R.

March 1980. Manatees from the Past. Fossils Found in Florida. *Fla. Conserv. News* 15 (6): 18–19.

Hogan, K.

1979. The Dugong: Plight of a Gentle Creature. *Aquasphere, J. New England Aquarium* 13 (2): 3–9.

Hussar, Sandra L.

1975a. The Dugong: endangered siren of the South Seas. *National Parks Conserv. Mag.*, Feb. 1975, 15–18.

1975b. A Review of the Literature of the Dugong (*Dugong dugon*). Washington, D.C.: U.S. Fish and Wildlife Serv., Wildlife Research Report 4, 1–30.

1977a. *Trichechus inunguis.* Amer. Soc. of Mammal., Mammalian Species No. 72: 1–4.

1977b. The West Indian Manatee (*Trichechus manatus*). Washington, D.C.: U.S. Fish and Wildlife Serv., Wildlife Research Report 7, 1–22.

1978a. *Dugong dugon.* Amer. Soc. of Mammal., Mammalian Species No. 88: 1–7.

1978b. *Trichechus senegalensis.* Amer. Soc. of Mammal., Mammalian Species No. 89: 1–3.

1978. *Trichechus manatus.* Amer. Soc. of Mammal., Mammalian Species No. 93: 1–5.

Irvine, A. Blair
    1983. Manatee Metabolism and Its Influence on Distribution in Florida.
    Biol. Conserv. 25 (4): 315–34.
Irvine, A. Blair, and H.W. Campbell
    1978. Aerial Census of the West Indian Manatee (*Trichechus manatus*) in the
    Southeastern United States. *J. Mammal.*, 59 (3): 613–17.
Irvine, A. Blair; H.W. Campbell; and D.K. Odell
    1977. Evidence for Seasonal Reproduction by the West Indian Manatee,
    Trichechus manatus. Abstracts, 1977 Annual Meeting, Amer. Soc. of Mam-
    mal., no. 164.
Irvine, A. Blair; D.K. Odell; and H.W. Campbell
    Manatee Mortality in the Southeastern United States, 1974–1977. Fla. Mar.
    Res. Pubs.
Jarman, P.J.
    1966. The Status of the Dugong (*Dugong dugon*) (Müller); Kenya, 1961. *East
    Afr. Wildl. J.* 4: 82–88.
Lee, Henry
    1883. *Sea Fables Explained.* London: Wm. Clower & Son.
Ligon, S.H.
    1976. A Survey of Dugongs (*Dugong dugon*) in Queensland. *J. Mammal.* 57
    (3): 580–82.
Loughman, W.D.; F.L. Frye; and E.S. Herald
    1970. The Chromosomes of a Male Manatee. *Intl. Zoo Yearb.* 10: 151–52.
Marmontal, Miriam
    1988. The Reproductive Anatomy of the Female Manatee, *Trichechus man-
    atus latirostris* (Linnaeus, 1758) Based on Gross and Historical Observa-
    tions. Master's thesis, Univ. of Miami.
Marsh, H.; G.E. Heinsohn; and A.V. Spain
    1978. The Physiology of the Dugong, *Dugong dugon. Comp. Biochem. Phys-
    iol.* 61A: 159–68.
Marsh, H.; T.J. O'Shea; and R.C. Best
    1986. Research on Sirenians. *Ambio.* 15 (3): 177–80.
Mondolphi, E.
    1973. Taxonomy, Distribution and Status of the Manatee in Venezuela.
    9pp. Manuscript.
Montgomery, G.G., and R.C. Best
    1979. Translocation and Stocking of the Amazonian Manatee, *Trichechus
    inunguis:* A Radiotelemetry Study. Proposal submitted to Smithsonian
    Scholarly Studies Program. 30pp.
Oberhen, J., and R. Prather
    Nov. 1979. Public Awareness Is Paying Dividends for an Endangered
    Species, The Federal Role. *Fla. Conserv. News* 15 (2): 6–9.

Odell, D.K.
  Dec. 1977. Age Determination and Biology of the Manatee. Final Report,
  Contract 14-16-0008-930, R.S.M.A.S. for U.S. Fish and Wildlife, Wash-
  ington, D.C. 122pp. Unpublished.
Odell, D.K.; D. Forrester; and E.D. Asper
  1978. Growth and Sexual Maturation in the West Indian Manatee. Ab-
  stracts, 1978 Annual Meeting, Amer. Soc. of Mammal.
Odell, D.K., and J.E. Reynolds
  1979. Observations on Manatee Mortality in South Florida. *J. Wildl. Mgmt.*
  43 (2) 572–77.
  March 1980. For West Indian Manatee, Collaborative Studies Beneficial.
  Fla. Conserv. News 15 (6): 4–5.
Odell, D.K.; J.E. Reynolds; and G. Wauch
  1978. New Records of the West Indian Manatee (*Trichechus manatus*) from
  the Bahama Islands. *Biological Conservation,* Applied Science Publ., Ltd.
  England 14: 289–93.
O'Shea, T.J.; C.A. Beck; R.K. Bonde; H.I. Kochman; and D.K. Odell
  1985. An Analysis of Manatee Mortality Patterns in Florida. *J. Wildl. Mgmt.*
  49 (1): 1–11.
Packard, J.M., and O.F. Wettergvist
  1986. Evaluation of Manatee Habitat Systems on the Northwestern Florida
  Coast. *J. Coastal Zone Mgmt.* 14 (4): 279–310.
Peterson, S.L.
  1974. Man's relationship with the Florida Manatee, *Trichechus manatus
  latirostris* (Harlan): an historical perspective. M.A. thesis, University of
  Michigan, Ann Arbor, Mich.
Phillips, Craig
  1964. *The Captive Sea.* Philadelphia, Pa.: Chilton.
Powell, J.A.
  1978. Evidence of Carnivory in Manatees (*Trichechus manatus*). *Mammal* 59
  (2): 442.
Powell, J.A., and G.B. Rathbun
  1984. Distribution and Abundance of Manatees along the Northern Coast
  of the Gulf of Mexico. *Northeast Gulf Science* 7 (1): 1–28.
Prather, R.
  March 1980. Manatee Protection Takes Joint Effort. *Fla. Conserv. News* 15
  (6): 6–7.
Rathbun, G.B., and J.A. Powell
  1983. Status of the West Indian Manatee in Honduras. *Biol. Conserv.* 26 (4):
  301–8.
Rathbun, G.A.; C.A. Woods; and J.A. Ottenwalder
  1985. The Manatee in Haiti. *Oryx* 19: 234–36.

Reeves, R.R.; D. Tuboku-Metzger; and R.A. Kapindi
   1988. Distribution and Exploitation of Manatees in Sierra Leone. *Oryx* 22
   (1): 75–84.
Reynolds, J.E.
   1976. The Florida Manatee, Myth vs Truth. *Sea Frontiers* 22 (4): 209–14.
   1977. Aspects of the Social Behavior and Ecology of Semi-isolated Colony
   of Florida Manatees (*Trichechus manatus*). Master's thesis, Univ. of Miami.
   Feb. 1979. The Semisocial Manatee. *Natural History* 88 (2): 44–53.
Reynolds, J.E., and D.K. Odell
   1977. Observations on Manatee Mortality Caused By Flood Control Dams
   in South Florida. Abstracts, 1977 Annual Meeting, Amer. Soc. of Mammal., no. 12.
   1991. *Manatees and Dugongs.* New York: Facts on File.
Reynolds, J.E., and J.R. Wilcox
   1986. Distribution and Abundance of the West Indian Manatee (*Trichechus
   manatus*) around Selected Florida Power Plants Following Winter Cold
   Fronts. *Biol. Conserv.* 38 (2): 103–13.
Ronald, K., and P.J. Healey
   1974. A Review of Sirens. College of Biol. Sci., Univ. of Guelph, Ontario,
   Canada. 31pp. Manuscript.
Roth, H.H., and E. Waitkuwait
   1986. Distribution and Status of Large Mammals in Ivory Coast. 3. Manatees. *Mammalia* 50 (2): 227–42.
Scheffer, V.B.
   1976. A Natural History of Marine Mammals. New York: Charles Scrib-
   ner's Sons.
Schevill, W., and W. Watkins
   1965. Underwater Calls of *Trichechus* (manatee). *Nature* (London) 205:
   373–74.
Scofield, John
   1975. Christopher Columbus and the New World He Found. *National
   Geographic* 148 (5): 584–625.
Sguros, P.L.
   1966. Research Report and Extension Proposal Submitted to the Central
   and Southern Florida Flood Control Board on Use of the Florida Manatee
   as an Agent for the Supression of Aquatic and Bankweed Growth in
   Essential Inland Waterways. Dept. Biol. Sci., Fla. Atl. Univ., Boca Raton.
   57pp. Manuscript.
Sguros, P.L.; T. Monkus; and C. Phillips
   1965. Observations and Techniques in the Study of the Florida Manatee—
   Reticent but Superb Weed Control Agent. 18th Annual Meeting of the
   Southern U.S. Weed Conf., Dallas, Texas.

Silveira, E.K. Pinto da
  1975. The Management of the Caribbean and Amazonian Manatees (*Trichechus manatus* and *T. inunguis*) in Captivity. *Intl. Zoo Yearbk.* 15: 223–26.
Steel, Cathy
  1982. Vocalization Patterns and Corresponding Behavior of the West Indian Manatee (*Trichechus manatus*). Ph.D. diss., Fla. Inst. of Tech., Orlando, Fla.
Steller, G.W.
  1751. De Bestiis Marinus. *Novi. Comm. Acad. Sci. Petropolitanae* (2): 289–398.
Tas'an, B.
  1976. Report on Catching and Life in Captivity of *Dugong dugon*. Jaya Ancol Oceanarium, Jakarta, Indonesia. 12pp.
Timm, R.M.; V. Albuja; and B.L. Clauson
  1986. Ecology, Distribution, Harvest and Conservation of the Amazonian Manatee (*Trichechus inunguis*) in Ecuador. *Biotropica* 18 (2): 150–56.
Twiss, J.R., Jr.
  1979. Manatee: Endangered Marine Mammal. *Water Spectrum* 12 (1): 10–17.
U.S. Fish and Wildlife Service
  1989. Florida Manatee (*Trichechus manatus latirostris*) Recovery Plan. Prepared by the Florida Manatee Recovery Team for the U.S. Fish and Wildlife Service, Atlanta, Ga. 98pp.
Vietmeyer, Noel D.
  1974. Endangered but Useful Manatee. *Smithsonian* 5: 60–65.
  Nov. 1975. The Beautiful Blue Devil. *Natural History* 84 (9): 65–72.
  1976. The Menaced Mermaid. *Science Year.* New York: World Book.
White, J.R.
  1970. Hematology and Blood Chemistry of the Florida Manatee. 6pp. Manuscript.
  1984. Born Captive, Released in the Wild. *Sea Frontiers* 30 (6): 369–70.
White, J.R.; D.R. Harkness; R.E. Isaacs; and D.A. Duffield
  1976. Some Studies on the Blood of the Florida Manatee, *Trichechus manatus latirostris*. *Comp. Biochem. Physiol.* 55A: 413–17.
Whitehead, P.J.P.
  1977. The Former Southern Distribution of the New World Manatees (*Trichechus* spp.). *Biol. J. Linn. Soc.* 9: 165–89.
  1978. Registros Antigos da Presenca do Peixe-Boi do Caribe (*Trichechus manatus*) do Brasil. *Acta Amazonica* 8 (3): 497–506.
Willis, C.
  Nov. 1979. Public Awareness Is Paying Dividends for an Endangered Species, the State's Role. *Fla. Conserv. News* 15 (2): 10–13.

Zeiller, W.
    1963. Sea Cow Parasitic Infestation. Special Report, Miami Seaquarium.
    5pp.
    1965. Care of a Young Manatee. Special Report, Miami Seaquarium. 5pp.
    1973. Florida Manatee: The Mutilated Species. *Fla. Conserv. Today,* May,
    p. 3.

Index ≋